God's Travel Advisory

God's Travel Advisory

On a Mission to South Sudan

Helen Miller

This Book is dedicated

To

the Lord Jesus Christ

who

has protected me,

or cushioned my fall

so many times,

I have lost count.

CONTENTS

Foreword   ix

Preface   x

Acknowledgments   xi

Introduction   1

PART I: MISSION DIARY

1. Avoid All Travel   5

2. Heaven Hotel   9

3. Getting Organized in Juba   13

4. Melut   21

5. On Standby in Melut   29

6. What Is Going On?   33

7. Plan B   41

8. Mission Possible: Juba   49

9. Take A Walk on The New Side   59

10 Finally, A Workshop!   65

11. Getting to Know the Neighbours   73

12. A Long Day   77

13. Sunday Morning   81

14. Sunday Afternoon   85

15. Exuberant Youth   89

16.	Day to Day Challenges	93
17.	Do Not Be Afraid. I Am Here.	103
18.	Changing Gears	109
19.	Another Workshop	115
20.	A Surprising Conclusion	119
21.	Departure	127
22.	Post-Juba	131

PART II: A MESSAGE FOR THE WEST

23.	West Meets East	139
24.	Why South Sudan?	147
25.	Re-Engineered Bucket Lists	153
26.	Is Peace Possible?	161
27.	Beyond Poverty and Politics – A Call to Action	167
28.	Are All Children Created Equal?	173
29	Removing the Stumbling Blocks	177
30	Removing Lampstands	191
Afterword		195
What About You?		196
Enquiries		199
One Last Thing		199

FOREWORD

Helen Miller has written a vivid, first-hand account of her mission trip to South Sudan. One feels that they are right there with her as she travels. The uncertainty and evacuation comes across very strongly. Helen makes a strong appeal for involvement in bible distribution, evangelism and compassion in this most needy, war-torn area. Your time will be well spent in reading this compelling book.

Rev. Dr. Ed Hird
St Simon's Church North Vancouver, BC.

Rev. Dr. Ed Hird is an author, columnist and blogger (https://edhird.com). His books include "The Battle for the Soul of Canada" and "Restoring Health: Body, Mind and Spirit".

PREFACE

In 2013, a tall man wearing a tunic or kaftan stood up in our workshop to make a point. He said, "people are not helping us." He pointed his long arm at me with his index finger extended saying, "You send a message to the West. We need help!"

Back at the hotel, in the slightly cooler part of the day, some of the men from the workshop came to visit me. They said, "we fought for 22 years for our freedom. We came out of the bush with nothing in our hands."

Upon returning to Canada, I wrote an article for a local newspaper, but there was no response. I travelled to South Sudan again in 2015 and after a somewhat eventful time with rebels active in the area, I decided to take my rough diary notes and record the daily events as a story about being on mission in an unpredictable place. After a few months, I came to the end of the story, but felt compelled to continue writing about South Sudan.

The book began to change direction, drawing attention to the difficult conditions that Christians are facing. It eventually broadens out to a wider appeal to the Christian church to step up and spend ourselves for Jesus Christ. We need all hands on deck to fulfill the Great Commission.

ACKNOWLEDGMENTS

This all began with an invitation from Chagai Lual of Padang Lutheran Relief Society in 2013. Chagai was one of the "Lost Boys" of Sudan who walked over 1,000 miles to find safety as a youth during the Second Sudanese Civil War (1983-2005). He originally came to Canada as a refugee and now gives back to his home country.

To those of you who donated funds to these missions to support South Sudan, please receive the heartfelt thanks of the people of South Sudan. When you give financial support, you're making a bold statement, firstly that you are intentional about fulfilling the Great Commission; secondly, that the money you are stewarding in your bank account is being used according to kingdom purposes and not according to the ways of the prince of this world. That's courageous, and a pleasing aroma to the Lord.

Those of you who prayed for these missions would know that you were all soldiers on duty under the leadership of the Captain of the Hosts of Heaven and that your service has been recorded in the books thereof. Even now as I think of all of you, I have a picture of one of you dressed in a soldier's uniform, back straight, arms flat at your sides, stepping up for duty. There is a discipline that is needed in battle and I see that in this amazing group of people.

When we are on the mission field, we can move about with relative confidence if we know that there is adequate prayer cover. It is not only for our benefit on the field, but for the protection of the local pastors and local churches. In July 2016, shortly before I left South Sudan, the pastors commented on how they knew they had been protected while we were there.

xi

There are several who encouraged, provided practical help and support, gave guidance at strategic junctures, challenged, prayed into specific issues, spoke prophetically or contributed in a significant and supernatural manner during the last 4 years. How divinely appointed you have been.

I want to acknowledge the pastors, leaders and local people of South Sudan (including the children) for their incredible welcome, participation, fellowship, and ministry. They have suffered greatly but continue to trust Jesus Christ.

I remember the faith and belief of my mother, my sister and my brother who acknowledged that this was a call to the mission field even though it looked a little different.

I want to thank my friend Daphne for her unwavering encouragement and prayerful prodding to finish this book.

INTRODUCTION

What do a barge full of rebels on the Nile River and a missing herd of cows pursued by a man with a gun have in common? Nothing really, except that they both represent the unpredictable nature of the mission field in places like South Sudan. Add to that thousands of displaced people sharing tents in temporary locations throughout the nation. Insecurity everywhere. Welcome to the new normal.

"God's Travel Advisory" begins with a true diarized account of a mission project in 2015 leading into a discussion about the critical nature of South Sudan and The Great Commission. The mission story reveals:

- A fledgling missionary grappling with cross-cultural situations;
- The reality of frustration and fear;
- The need for endurance and flexibility;
- The discovery of a well of compassion;
- Some pitfalls to avoid; and,
- Wisdom along the way.

The second part, "A Message for the West" will lead the reader to wrestle with questions that emerge, such as:

- Why is South Sudan strategic in the overall scheme of things in continental Africa?
- Why should Christians help the churches of South Sudan?
- Can a culture of revenge be changed?
- How can churches evangelize in a climate of insecurity?
- Are foreign missionaries welcome in South Sudan?

- Are tribal ties stronger than the gospel?
- Does God send missionaries to dangerous places?
- Are overseas missions taking a new direction?
- Should I repurpose my bucket list?
- Should I have a bucket list?
- How have children been traumatized?
- Can we ignore the cry of brothers and sisters in other nations?
- How do we pray for our churches to be "missional"?

Chapter 29 turns from South Sudan in particular and grapples with the wider fears and concerns that seem to cripple our responses to the call of our missional God. Chapter 30 issues a fresh call to reap the harvest.

The ultimate point to this book is not a travel story or doing good works. It is about a God who is sovereign and who wants us to trust Him with our lives. It is only the knowledge of Him and the understanding of how He has guided us that allows one to go to a conflicted place like South Sudan.

I hope that this book inspires you to trust God more, and that you will put your faith in Jesus Christ to the point of placing your whole life in His hands. I believe that when you do that, when you can let go of all that the world offers, you will find your true life in Him.

PART I

MISSION DIARY

1
Avoid All Travel

We boarded the transit bus at Dubai Airport Terminal # Two, a motley crew of people travelling to Juba, South Sudan for a range of reasons. A conversation began loosely amongst a handful of us as strangers. One man announced that he detected landmines for a living and could not wait for his contract to end. "Who would want to go to Juba anyway?" he asked. "Why would anyone want to go to Juba!", like it was the worst place on earth. The man next to me said it was related to his work. The landmine detector turned to me next. "And you?"

I thought it best to simply say "missionary and humanitarian work".

He lost interest after that. It was the obvious answer. Why else would anyone go to Juba intentionally? Who else is crazy enough to go? When I lived in Papua New Guinea years ago, I heard people say only misfits, missionaries and mercenaries lived in places like that. Rascal gangs used to attack expatriates, rob them, rape their wives and so forth. One day, people began to turn cars over and set them on fire outside of Parliament House which was not far from where I worked. We locked down our compound until the antics had stopped. Juba sounded like it had the same reputation.

I had first visited Juba in October 2013 on my way to Malakal. Juba was a gateway and a stepping stone to where I needed to go. It was never intended to be a place where I would stay for more than a night or two. The Canadian government travel advisories announced in red, over-sized letters "AVOID ALL TRAVEL". Juba was a place to avoid because of its propensity for violent crime not to mention the coming and going of military leaders of opposing forces. The war that began in December 2013 had divided the country along ethnic lines. Despite several attempts at reconciliation, the President and ex-Vice President were still fighting.

Fighting in South Sudan had a long history. Much of the tribal infighting in provinces like Jonglei appeared to be over cattle rustling and territorial encroachment. Cattle were a very valuable commodity. Unfortunately, there did not seem to be a justice system between tribes that ensured that punishment fitted the particular crime and so fighting and killing appeared to be the standard response to solving these problems once and for all.

However, it was not only the cattle that were valuable. The oilfields in the Upper Nile region were a strategic target for those who wished to create mayhem at a national and international level. There was only one operating refinery left near Paloich in the north. The revenue from this facility funded the government of South Sudan's military. Local South Sudanese said that arms were regularly transported from Sudan through the town of Kodok, by the Nile River to the rebel forces (officially known as SPLA-IO).[1]

When I visited Malakal in 2013, the locals would sit under the trees in plastic chairs in the cool of the afternoon (if there is such a thing as a cool temperature there) and tell me their stories. The main theme that emerged from those times was "you tell the people of the West...we came out of the bush [after fighting for freedom] with nothing in our hands. No-one is helping us. We need help."

---

[1]. Sudan People's Liberation Army – In Opposition.

Some of these men had given up 22 years of their lives to fight for what they believed in. Prior to the internal power struggle that started in 2013, their people had endured two previous civil wars. A brief history lesson might help here. After independence in 1956, Britain handed Sudan over to an Arab Muslim government in Khartoum. The people of the south (who were mostly not Muslim) declared civil war when it became apparent that power was not being shared with them. The war lasted twenty-two years until the Addis Ababa peace agreement of 1972.

In 1983, the Sudanese government imposed Sharia Law in Sudan, which ignited a second uprising by the south, led by Dr. John Garang, founder of the Sudan People's Liberation Army. Ironically, he fought for Sudan to remain a unified country and accused the government of marginalizing certain groups in Darfur. (Local sources told me of their stories of discrimination and persecution in Khartoum. Christians were thrown into prison, denied work or generally harassed.)

In 2005, the Sudanese Comprehensive Peace Agreement was signed but the arrangements soon disintegrated. According to the local Dinka people, the various agreements allowing the southern population to be involved in consultation were not honoured. In 2011, the independent nation of South Sudan finally emerged. A high price had been paid in blood for such freedom. The fighting however has continued with the Sudanese government over territorial boundaries and oil wealth sharing. From independence, South Sudan was like an infant in an incubator, needing special care to ensure that it thrived. Its adversary lay in wait for another opportunity to strike. Could this child survive the odds?

2
Heaven Hotel

Touching down at Juba airport, I saw the familiar sight of United Nations (UN) cargo planes, commercial planes and an assortment of small NGO[2] aircraft and UN helicopters. What was new was the white UN tent testing for the Ebola virus. We were hustled into the tent directly off the tarmac to complete forms. I sat at a small table to complete mine and was asked several times if I was a member of the UN staff to help passengers to complete their forms. Soon my pen was borrowed by a passerby. Then an illiterate woman had me writing out her sketchy identification details. As soon as she disappeared, I stepped into the line before anyone else asked for help. The white temperature monitor soon clicked over my forehead and I was clear to go.

I stepped into line for my passport to be stamped. I waited an hour in the stifling heat before the line moved one step. Sudanese men in their suits pushed to the front of the line and waved their passports under the noses of border officials. This patience-stretching exercise seemed to set the tone of the whole mission from day one. An Indian expatriate man urged me twice to go to the head of the line and to push my passport forward. I pondered that. How would it look for a white woman, a Christian missionary to push her way to the front of the line for preferential treatment? I waited and then switched lines. You know how it goes. As

---

2. NGO: A non-governmental organization is a non-profit organization that is independent from states and international governmental organizations.

soon as you think you have changed to a better lane, the other traffic moves faster. Finally, a Sudanese official (either at the request of the Sudanese people who were patiently waiting for me, or out of pity for this naïve visitor) took my passport and led me to the front of the line. I was almost at the end of my tether. (My mother used to say that when she was frustrated. She was an avid horse rider as a young girl.). We loaded my luggage into a van borrowed from a pastor's uncle. It was a happy reunion with the Sudanese people. I had three suitcases, one for my personal effects, one full of humanitarian packages of dried soup mix to make 1,800 cups plus second hand clothes for children, and a third suitcase full of mostly children's Bible school program supplies (face paint for 350 faces, a baseball set, bubbles and wands, plastic balls for games, 8 Canadian beach balls, Bible school materials and lessons, 3 water filters, 30 custom made bags for youth leaders, specially designed record cards for 300 children, 1,500 stickers, stationery and so on.) If anyone was ready, I was. I had spent quite a lot of time shopping, packing and weighing to ensure everything would be useful and the bags would not be overweight.

The name of the hotel made me smile, "Heaven Hotel". It reminded me of the Father's care as well as His sense of humour. The people at my church who were praying for this mission would delight in such things and it was a trail of signs yet to come. When I left Canada for Juba via Seattle the day before, I almost missed the onward Emirates flight from Seattle to Dubai. I was sitting away from the actual boarding gate thinking I had plenty of time when suddenly I heard a final boarding call. I ran to the gate and handed over my boarding pass and passport. The man shook his head and said, "You need to have your passport verified." Almost everyone else was on the plane and two others were boarding ahead of me. I went to the desk. The airline staff were asking for receipts for my luggage. A Middle Eastern man in a smart-looking suit stood next to me, turned to me with a smile and said in a clear, calm voice, "Ma'am, don't worry. We will take good care of you." A new document was prepared for my luggage receipt. My passport was verified. I was the last passenger to enter the boarding tunnel. Halfway along the tunnel to the plane door, two customs officials caught up with me. There was also a man in a wheelchair waiting to board the plane. After answering a few questions, we were released to travel. I had to sign a form to clear the issue, but by now, my hand was shaking a great deal so I could barely manage a chicken scratch. As I turned to walk toward the door, the Middle Eastern man appeared by my side again and said, "Don't worry Ma'am. We will take good care of you." Who was that man?

I boarded the flight and finally took a seat. I was both bemused by all the kafuffle of trying to board this flight and sobered by the near miss. Was I the most incompetent missionary of all time or am I jumping through a lot of hoops here for a good reason? Over the PA system came the captain's welcome with an Australian accent. It sounded professional, but relaxed and friendly.

With 14 hours of flight time I decided to review the list of movies and programs available. I recalled "Unbroken"[3] had been commended as a noble film-making endeavour. This movie set me up for what lay ahead with a mantra that I repeated over and over in my mind when things were going sideways. Louie Zamporini was constantly in trouble as a young boy and so his ability to run fast proved to be an asset at an early age. His older brother, seeing his potential began

---

[3]. Film, *Unbroken*, Directed by Angelina Jolie, 2014.

to coach him as an athlete and said to him, "If you can take it, you can make it."

Zamporini qualified for his first Olympics and headed off to compete. As the train pulled out of the station, Louie's brother said, "A moment of pain is worth a lifetime of glory, remember that."

Years later, the young man, now an American Olympic athlete was in a Japanese prisoner of war camp. The commander who seeks to break the spirit of the American instructed him to lift a heavy beam of timber over his head and hold it there indefinitely. The American succeeded in holding up the beam until it was the Japanese commander who broke down, confounded by the American's ability to endure several acts of unspeakable cruelty. If the young American athlete, Zamporini could take it, he could make it, indeed.

Meanwhile, back in Juba, room 114 featured a double bed with a mosquito net with a pretty frill around the edge. The plumbing worked (unlike in war-torn Malakal in 2013) and there was even an air conditioner and lo and behold a television set mounted high up on the wall adjacent to the bed. The price was reasonable and the place had a level of security that was acceptable with razor wire and a locked entrance at night. Vehicles were crammed into the central courtyard each night and no-one could go in or out. I went downstairs and rounded up the person who appeared to be the cook. She was from Eritrea and did not speak English so we cornered Ali (I think that was his name or close enough) who spoke sufficient English to sort out a menu: spaghetti, macaroni or "cheeken and cheaps" (chicken and chips) as I heard it.

Chagai, the Executive Director of Padang Lutheran Relief Society (PLRS) and I agreed to head to immigration the next morning to take care of formalities.

3
Getting Organized in Juba

At the immigration department the next day, we found a mixture of nationals and foreigners standing around trying to process paperwork, waiting for long periods. We asked around and discovered that I needed a form. The way to get this form was to knock on a window and interrupt a young woman in a tiny office space and ask for it. It came back via a long arm through an awkward, narrow opening. I completed the form and found that I now needed to walk around the corner to a small window adjacent to the last one, same office, and same person. I stood in line with some Sudanese gentlemen at this window. Interestingly, there was a small garden at this window. We had no choice but to stand in the garden, side-stepping plants.

The way to get your paperwork processed was to thrust your arm through the open window with your paperwork in hand and wave it there for attention. We stood in the hot sun like this for some time. Finally, we paid a fee and then proceeded to someone else's office. They looked at the paperwork, approved it and then opened a file. This man sent us to see the army officers sitting at computers in the back room. They looked at the documents and said I had not completed the form correctly. I needed a passport photo and a photocopy of the document. We organized the photocopy and meanwhile I dug out a spare passport photo which was several years old. I looked completely different and a lot younger but nobody raised an eyebrow about that. It was a photo. All white people probably looked the same to them. No big deal. I sometimes have the same problem with people of other cultures, unless I have spent time with them personally...but then I have trouble remembering everyone these days. We then went into the office of the senior officer who approved the documentation and we were on our way. This took most of the morning.

We headed to a cellphone network provider for credit on our phones and organized a 3G internet stick. This too took a while. Patience was the name of the game. I had to let go of expectations of anything going the way I thought it should. The new normal was to just do the next thing however long it took. If it cannot be done today it will have to wait until ...whenever. I didn't recall having to wait so long for everything last time, but then, this mission had four times the budget and was more complex. We were venturing into bigger things and engaging the local organizations and stores on a daily basis, doing business and building relationships with the storekeepers. I had to learn to close my mouth and not express frustration or annoyance. There were cultural expectations that could never be met and it was futile to say anything about them.

A projector had been put aside for us in a store in Juba town, so we spent time there testing the laptop that I brought with the projector and soon discovered that the laptop needed an upgrade to work successfully. A woman at my church had donated the computer which was about 2006 vintage. The tech-savvy store owner said he would take care of it and by the time we returned, everything was functioning.

About mid-afternoon, the heat and long periods of waiting had taken their toll. I returned to the hotel to take a rest. The generator was working and the electricity was now on. It was usually switched off at 7.00 am each day and resumed around 2.00 pm. I checked email briefly and noticed a travel alert from the United States which said:

14

"Country Travel Risk Level: Extreme
There are reports of increasing violence in Unity
State. Many international organizations have withdrawn their staff from the region, and the U.S. Embassy advises U.S. citizens in the area to depart immediately." [4]

I skimmed this and immediately a wave of fear came over me. It was overwhelming. I thought I could not bear the weight of it. I prayed and then laid down for a few hours. It was so hot. I had no energy. The air conditioner worked between 8.00 pm and 1.00 am only. I knew what the travel advisories said before I came. So did the Lord, yet he still sent me here. How could I doubt his protection now? *(Please especially read "Afterword" at the end of this book.)*

I decided to email for prayer as our travel and cargo plans were not finalized. I felt for a while that afternoon a certain despair and hopelessness.

The next day, Thursday May 14, we continued to move forward. A Sudanese man wearing a uniform and sunglasses met us that day. We made our way to an office at the airport and left the two suitcases of supplies there. I had labelled each suitcase with vivid yellow duct tape with the name "Padang Lutheran Relief Society" and described the contents so there was no mistake as to what these were for. There was a place to eat nearby so the three of us went in for a meal. It was now afternoon and none of us had eaten all day.

While Chagai was busy elsewhere, Pastor Jack and I chatted. He told me about his work escorting visiting mission teams. He said one team leader complained and chastised him so much for not adhering exactly to their schedule, it made him "sick". He sounded thoroughly disgusted by the

---

[4] Please see my comments on travel advisories at the end of this book under "Afterword" for clarification.

way he was treated. Pastor Jack did have a habit of arriving late or taking detours to do other things. My observation was that the time that he arrived was perhaps what the Holy Spirit intended. I found that when I was willing to be flexible and allowed the situation to roll along, it worked out in the end, without the bad feeling of having condemned the driver for his perceived untimeliness. When we badger and browbeat a people who have been raised with a markedly different understanding of time, community and priorities, we destroy rather than build up. Our words become but clanging symbols in their ears and relationships become soured.[5]

We also visited the Commissioner of Baliet County, James Torr that day at the New York Hotel. I met James in Malakal in October 2013 on my first foray into South Sudan. He was staying at the same hotel and was having an outdoor meeting with his staff on plastic chairs (as you do) in the hotel courtyard. I was introduced to him and instantly liked him. He was very personable and accessible as a leader and graciously gave me a few minutes of his time.

So here we were again, taking tea in Juba this time. He welcomed us and made a short speech of thanks for our efforts. In between calls and messages on his two cellphones, we talked about the bullet that is still lodged in his arm along with the screws and metal implanted through surgeries in Nairobi. I looked at the X-ray on his cellphone fascinated by it all. When fighting broke out in December 2013, James

---

[5] I believe that the Lord of the Harvest is calling all cultures to work together in a new way, a way that will bring great joy. It will require an adjustment of intercultural communication on the part of every tongue, nation and tribe. This will be challenging, but has the potential to unleash internationally the kind of love that we have all longed to experience in the body of Christ, especially within our own churches.

stayed in Malakal to protect women and children and literally took a bullet for his people. He stood firm. When I was preparing to go to Malakal in September 2013 the Lord gave me a message for the leaders there. It was to say that they should not run away like a hired hand at the first sign of trouble. James is a hero in the eyes of his people. He has great support from them because of his courage. I think he could be described as an elder-statesman in South Sudan. He was hoping for a further surgery in Germany soon so I prayed for his arm and his work and we bid good-bye.

Hoping for a seat on a flight to the oil fields, we paid a visit to an oil company office the next day. Our names had been registered previously, but the paperwork was missing so now our names could not be included on the waitlist. Chagai searched through a large pile of papers several times. He went to an adjoining office looking for a way around this but there was no joy there either. He returned and went over the paperwork one more time with a staff member and finally located what he needed. We were told to wait and see as the flight was fully occupied. Our window of hope lay in the possibility that two company personnel could potentially fail to check in by 4.30pm that day (and lose their seats). That would give us the required tickets and that is exactly what happened. God is good.

On the way home, we stopped at a market to buy a small suitcase. We were limited to 15 kg of baggage on the charter flight. Chagai led the way into a store. We tried to bargain but the price was not budging. I wanted to see what else was available and to compare the prices so we went into a more crowded market where the corridors were very narrow. We stopped to look at some bags, but Chagai seemed ill at ease. He said we should leave. I was not comfortable with the closeness of everything and there seemed to be mostly men around the market. I followed him immediately without question. We hurried out of the market and returned to the first storekeeper. A price was agreed and we left soon after with a black suitcase featuring a built-in combination lock. On Friday morning May 15, we headed for Juba airport. I had vomited that morning and had diarrhoea at the hotel but trusted I would feel better. The anti-malaria tablets were upsetting my stomach. I lined up with a throng of people trying to enter through a narrow doorway to the single departure lounge for this international airport. Awash in a sea of black faces. I must have looked like a piece of flotsam, a white pasty piece of debris floating along toward a narrow water tunnel to be discharged as waste. Still feeling queasy, I noticed that the pastor who drove us to the airport was still there. He said "Helen, if you're not well, you don't have to fly today." I thought of the words of Zamporini's brother "if you can take it, you can make it." I said, "It will be okay" and stayed in line moving forward slowly. Then the unthinkable happened. The last remaining contents of my stomach were on their way up like an elevator that had only one destination. I panicked inwardly in the next two seconds and all I could think of was "use your hat".

My poor hat. It was a white panama style hat with the black headband that had a touch of elegance to it from the Le Chateau store in Canada. This was about to become a dumping ground, and so it was. I squashed the hat around my mouth quickly and then kept it firmly in my grasp with its earthy contents until I passed through the narrow doorway, through the security screening process and then onto a women's washroom. How I managed to handle a backpack, a bulging tote bag, a passport, a boarding pass and an elegant looking sick bag I don't recall.

I found in the washroom a large metal drum which probably carried fuel once. It was full of water with some Dettol

18

disinfectant in it. The water was murky with random unidentified floating contents. Without thinking too much about it, I plunged the hat into the liquid abyss and washed it as clean as it could be. It was hoped that the hat would soon dry and that no-one would even know what happened at Juba airport. What happens at the airport stays at the airport. I began to feel better. I probably had little protection against malaria at this point but would start that process off again the next day. Onward ho!

4
Melut

Our one-armed friend James met us at the airport at Paloich with a driver and vehicle. James's arm was amputated after he was shot during the war that led to South Sudan's independence in 2011. There was no support for war veterans in South Sudan as we have in other nations. In fact, there was no formal recognition or acknowledgement of the plight of people like James who fought for the freedom of all South Sudanese. He met us with his usual smile and warm handshake. The weather was hot and dry and breathless. We bundled into the vehicle and then drove straight onto the tarmac. There were no rules here. You could drive close to the stationary aeroplanes as if you were about to refuel them. Cargo planes were unloading onto the ground. We could see my two suitcases sitting in the shadow of the aircraft waiting for us.

The drive to Melut was dusty and thirsty on a gravel road under construction for improvement by the local oil company. Trucks went to and fro. People walked long distances along the road as they could not afford transport. It was the UN, the government and the NGOs who had passenger vehicles here. We arrived at Melut town which was a sparsely built area of tukels[6] and old compound accommodation along with a small market and a few places that one might call cafes or restaurants and lodgings. I lay down on a bed in a tin shed with an old fan whirring to and fro. I could not tell if it was better to sit outside in a bit of shade or to lay on the bed in front of the fan. Either option was a slow roast. Later,

---

6. Thatch-roofed huts.

we visited a compound belonging to a theological college. The person we thought we should speak to was not there and so we wondered what to do. God always has a plan. We paused. A sprightly woman wearing a skirt, blouse and a lua[7] over her shoulder accessorized with a bandana around her forehead gave us a kind smile and welcome. This was Karen the missionary nurse. She had 20 years of experience in Ethiopia and was the "go to" person for all things mission, at least for me.

Before long, I was moving luggage into the spare room which Karen called her "project room" equipped with small bar fridge, fan, pantry and water filter along with a bed and cupboard. I was now the project. The nausea from early in the morning had developed into an internal condition that I had some years ago. With one tablet and the ongoing prayer of the saints back home, it resolved within 24 hours. There are any number of things that can go wrong in a situation like this. I reminded myself daily that God had sent me here and that He knew every detail. This was enough to keep me calm and positive that things would work out. The prophetic word from a man at our church about preparing to go on this mission was also an invaluable encouragement. I recalled it from time to time to shore up the sides of my mindset about what we were doing in this place that was being abandoned like a hot potato.

My sponsor brought a young woman named "Achol" to the house to help with any chores. She appeared to be in her late teens. No-one discussed this with me. However, I did

---

7 · A "lua" is a piece of colourful fabric draped across a woman's body and tied over one shoulder. It is usually worn over a t-shirt or blouse and gives an elegant and modest appearance for women.

not challenge it. Before I left Canada, a man said that he believed God would send a young woman to me and that I was to bless her. He said it may seem a small thing to me, but it was something that the Lord wanted to do. I was happy to meet Achol. I liked her instantly. She was eager to work. She asked me on more than one occasion what she could do to help. I asked Achol if she could wash some clothes. She tackled this with gusto, lifting shirts high out of a bowl of soapy water and plunging them back in for a second scrub. She was good at laundry. I was impressed by the clean and neat presentation of the Sudanese. The men seemed to wear crisp clean shirts and nice shoes while I limped along in not quite matching pieces and simple shoes that did the job.

Karen's water filters were remarkable pieces of equipment. Achol topped them up for me from the tap in the backyard. The water trickled from the top compartment through cylinders containing a material of gravel consistency into a lower chamber. It tasted quite good. By now, Chagai and our friend James Chagai had arrived. We headed to the market in the heat of the day. Only "mad dogs and Englishmen" go out in the midday sun, but there we were baking in the middle of a flat, forlorn landscape. As we walked along the road, a vehicle stopped and from it emerged a pastor we met in Malakal in 2013. Every day, the impact of displacement was seen and felt. The whole country had been scrambled. No-one seemed to live in their homes anymore. No-one felt safe.

We continued on to the local market and bought some rice and pasta, onions, garlic, oil and salt. That was about all I could find that I could cook easily as a meal. There was a kind of instant noodle that was suggested for breakfast so I bought that too. We paid for a boy and his donkey to haul our small grocery purchase of 10 kg of rice and other items on a cart. This was an efficient form of transport. I liked the idea of being able to pay them for this service. There were no jobs here except for the government workers and the oil-field workers so any gainful employment was a good thing. However, I wondered about the donkeys. I felt so sad for animals that had no medical care. When the donkeys brayed loudly it sounded like a distress signal. I had to get used to that.

Achol returned at 4.00 pm. I gave her the job of cooking some rice. I had not had a meal for almost a day now (surviving on some almonds and a granola bar) so this was a good start - rice, garlic and onions fried in oil. The Sudanese tended not to worry about quantities too much. I guess when you live in a village, you cook for more than yourself as normal practice. Although I had already halved the quantity that Achol was about to tip into the boiling water, we still produced a large amount. While Achol only ate a small portion, I savoured the rice and probably reeked of garlic afterwards. I began to understand why NGO's talked about "food security". When one cannot buy more than a little food at the market, and the land is not producing crops, there is a creeping fear that our hunger may never be satisfied. It brings a feeling of vulnerability and insecurity, day by day. Not knowing. Imagine how hungry children (or the mother of hungry children) can be manipulated.

Alex, the regional coordinator for PLRS, along with the man in the sunglasses who helped us with cargo, and Chagai came to discuss what assistance we needed to run a workshop and a children's program. Afterwards, we met the leaders of a local church. They were meeting under a tree by the Nile River. We approached and were invited to sit with them. I shared what we were offering to do and they seemed agreeable.

There was talk about rebels in the region. The team leader of the college came by while Alex was there. He had met with the UN and decided that it was not necessary to arrange evacuation at this time. However, people were saying that the recent relocation of the governor and the commissioner to Melut might attract rebels here. These were rumours. It seemed so peaceful here by the Nile. People went about their domestic chores and visited one another. Tea was sipped. The youth from Melut and from Paloich had been singing and playing keyboards and drums in the church all day and into the night. I tried to sleep under the mosquito net with the windows and doors closed, sweltering. It was only the second day here and it felt like a week had passed by.

The next morning, Karen and I headed to the church nearby. I had been up early reading the book of Numbers and simultaneously asking God what I would say to the congregation that morning as a visiting worker. I was reading the passage where God says to Moses that he had not treated the Lord as holy and this was a matter of disobedience. I wrote a short message of a few paragraphs about disobedience and the impact on our intimate relationship with the Father. The message ended with a note about obedience including the notion of a relationship, not just obeying a set of rules. It is relationship that the Father desires. I shared this brief message with the assistance of a faulty microphone and a shy translator who was a little unsure of what I was trying to convey. Never mind. I delivered it as best I could.

The leaders announced that our evangelism workshop would take place starting Wednesday and everyone was welcome. There was exuberant worship for hours featuring the youth from two congregations, one from Paloich and one from Melut. The sides of the church building were comprised of sheet metal which could be opened out in 2 places like large windows. There was a slight breeze for which we were all grateful. Finally, the service ended. It started with a prayer meeting at 8.00 am and ended about 1.00 pm.

I was glad of a rest in the afternoon. Hunger finally took over. Earlier in the day, Karen had generously surrendered a can of Spam of my choice – smoked turkey flavour or pork. I chose the turkey flavour and chopped it into oil in a frying pan on a small electric burner on the floor. It seemed incongruous that there would be electricity here, but I understood that it was part of the oil industry's infrastructure that we were enjoying. Later, some leftover rice, onion and garlic was added with half a stock cube for flavour. I was glad of some protein and a sense of fullness from a meal. This was almost gourmet. Fried Spam. Who would have thought?

In those moments, I appreciated the difficulty of trying to ship supplies like Spam along with water filters and other equipment with the meagre baggage allowances on airlines. It truly was kind of Karen to share her treasured pantry stocks, some of which were gifts to her as specialty items. She personally was such a gift to me and everyone else. What an amazing and genteel woman...a seasoned worker in the field who had remedies for snakebite and an ingenious rig for taking a solar powered shower. This was quite something. Who knew that one could have a hot shower in the middle of nowhere? Even at the Heaven Hotel in Juba there were no hot showers.

About 4.30 pm, a message came that the team leader of the college staff wanted to update me on a recent development. Malakal had been taken by the rebel forces. Apparently, there had been an earlier attack by some Shilluk rebels. This caused all the local Shilluk who were not part of this rebellion to run away for fear of retaliation by the other tribes. The Shilluk rebels then joined the mainstream Nuer rebel forces.

The combined rebel army were reported to be making their way north of Malakal, but another report indicated that the SPLA were fighting to re-take the city. Fear sprang up as if it had been waiting for this opportunity to show itself. I went over to the team leader's house and listened. The staff had a 5.00 pm Bible study and prayer time, so I stayed for that and we prayed about the situation. During the worship that morning, Karen said a passage from 2 Chronicles came to mind. King Jehoshaphat and all of Judah were faced with a vast army so he prayed to the Lord God, "For we have no power to face this vast army that is attacking us. We do not know what to do, but our eyes are on you" (2 Chronicles 20:12).

I could not believe that God would have me come all this way to be evacuated. After lumping those three suitcases to Melut with provision of flights and cargo and preparing as the Lord had directed, I could not see the sense of this. No-one wanted to evacuate. We were all poised to do work and this was so inconvenient and frustrating. Decisions had to be made. Apparently, there had been three alerts in recent times and nothing had transpired, but we had to wait and see what developed overnight. My host had said that Akoka was where the line was drawn. If the rebels should reach that place, that was our signal to move for sure. I had no idea where Akoka was. The maps I had viewed did not indicate its whereabouts, but it had to be north of Malakal near the river.

Meanwhile, at the prayer meeting, a hymn came to Karen's mind:

> Day by day and with each passing moment
>
> Strength I find to meet my trials here
>
> Trusting in my Father's wise bestowment
>
> I've no cause for worry or for fear.

I recalled it from our Sunday night prayer group meetings in Canada. We would briefly discuss an old hymn each week, delving into the author's motives for writing the song and the meaning behind the wonderful lyrics. Many of the great hymns were born of difficult circumstances and the hymn "Day by Day" was one of them. When she was 26 years of age, Lina Sandell [8] took a boat ride across a lake to Gothenburg in Sweden. During the trip, her father, a Lutheran pastor, fell overboard and drowned before her eyes. Following this tragedy Lina wrote many hymns from a broken heart.

---

[8]. Full name: Karolina Wilhelmina Sandell-Berg, (3 October 1832–27 July 1903). Lyrics quoted were translated by Andrew L. Skoog. The hymn's tune was composed in 1872 by Oscar Ahnfelt. See www.hymnary.org; also see Wikipedia.https://en.wikipedia.org.

5
On Standby in Melut

On Monday morning, May 18, Chagai arrived around 9.00 am and we discussed recent developments and the fall of Malakal. The SPLA[9] reportedly began to bomb the town last night. The rebels held two barges and had strategically parked one of them near the UN base. At that time, the SPLA were still on the outside of the city, but the Dinka thought that they would soon receive reinforcements and take back the strategic centre of Malakal. The army needed to destroy both of the rebel barges on the river. Another story we heard was that the army had taken a barge also and was making its way down from the north to meet the rebels, but experienced mechanical trouble and had to return to Renk overnight for repairs. The bombing expedition against the rebels also experienced technical difficulty.

The driver came and took a few of us to the camp for internally displaced people (IDP), not far away. I tried to video the drive but it was very bumpy and dusty. We walked around the camp and came to the IDP community school where the children had just been released for a break. We had a meeting with the local school teachers. They were young and received a pittance for their work, but they were willing to teach the children what they knew. Some had been trained as teachers by "Open Door" at Yei while others had

---

9. Sudan People's Liberation Army is the army of the Republic of South Sudan. The SPLA was founded as a guerrilla movement in 1983 and was a key participant of the Second Sudanese Civil War. Throughout the war, it was led by John Garang de Mabior. https://en.wikipedia.org. (Wikipedia).

no formal training. The school was funded by the small enrolment fees paid by parents. There were 740 children attending. Their class sizes for grades one to eight were as follows:

1. 131
2. 89
3. 109
4. 99
5. 90
6. 73
7. 59
8. 94

There were many more children in the camp not attending. Some fathers did not see the value of education and did not understand what it was, being illiterate themselves. Others simply did not have the money (a few dollars per month).

Six blackboards and some exercise books had been sent by a small NGO, but the boards were a little small for the teachers to use effectively. They hired four plastic chairs from a local storekeeper for their office furniture. I made a list of what would be helpful to them, with plastic sheeting taking priority. A plastic sheet over the roof of each classroom would enable children to attend school when it rained. It would only cost a few dollars but needed to be shipped in from Juba most likely. They needed exercise books, pens, text books and sporting equipment and some support for the teachers to live on. They showed me one text book, a small soft cover science book. That appeared to be all they had. I asked if I could pray for them and their needs and they all bowed their heads. We left feeling confident that we could do something to help them.

I was very surprised to see a couple of stores in the camp, like a mini market. There was stationery, clothing and some food for sale. Very few could afford these items. One person was selling a small amount of sorghum laid out on a sheet on the ground but I didn't see any takers. I bought a pen and a mango drink mix from Sudan that had enough neon orange food colouring in it to dye a t-shirt. It provided a welcome change to plain water. The storekeeper seemed happy to have a customer.

We saw a vegetable patch that people in the camp had been tending. A vegetable like okra was growing quite well on the river bank. They watered it by hand. We also saw women cooking leaves from a tree. There had been no food distribution by any organization since March 2015 and so people would simply eat these cooked leaves to fill their stomachs. The camp residents were generally despondent and hungry. Two leaders talked to us briefly. There was not a lot to say: "Our people are suffering". They looked at the ground as they talked. We all looked at the ground. Hope for them was almost gone. It hardly seemed worthwhile talking about the need. Why waste the energy? I felt useless but remembered that I cannot solve every problem I see. I empathized with the suffering. It seemed so hard. "Lord, why is this happening to these people?"

6
What Is Going On?

Mid-afternoon, Karen advised that her team were preparing to evacuate the next day. They were guided by their organization's evacuation protocol, but with some discretion as to timing and options. As a guest of the relief society, I trusted in my host's advice and ability to know when and how to move in this situation. He was aware of the options. I also knew that my host was led of the Lord by the same Holy Spirit. There have been so many occasions, too numerous to mention, where Chagai and I have come to the same conclusion on the many issues that arise on the mission field. We part in the afternoon after discussing a matter with questions in our minds. The next day, we are finishing each other's sentences with the same solution in mind. God is so good and I am so grateful for the prayers of the people at home. They have provided the covering that allows this unity of spirit to gel amidst challenging circumstances. No matter what problems we have faced on the field, there has always been a solution or a way forward or a way out. Sometimes we have missed God's signpost, but He has graciously mitigated the situation in some way.

Not one of us wanted to leave, yet there was something in the air. I remember feeling unsettled. I began to walk to the UN base. Achol came part way with me and then departed for home. I continued on alone thinking this was not an ideal situation but I needed to press on. I noticed how people were packing a few possessions and either heading to the base or heading for Paloich on foot with family in tow. I called Chagai and agreed to wait for him outside of the base. As I stood outside of the gate, I noticed a utility truck drive by equipped with a mounted machine gun and a man in civilian clothing standing behind it. They appeared to be headed for Paloich. The modern version of the Wild West perhaps?

We met with Edward, the Head of Security for the United Nations Mission in South Sudan (UNMISS) for the Upper Nile. He was emphatic that there would be shelling and gunfire (from the rebels) in Melut that night and that we should come to the base. He said that they would not allow troops to go out and bring people to the UN camp later tonight. I noticed that there were two tanks inside the gates of the compound with guns pointed toward the Nile River. Further, he said to Chagai, "You are South Sudanese. You should have told her [as a foreigner working with an NGO] about this. Why didn't you tell her?" I am not sure what he meant. We had already discussed possible evacuation. He was making a big issue of this. Had something been withheld from me that my host should be chastised in this way? I didn't think so. The difference here was that we had the spirit of God guiding us. There was no panic about evacuation at this moment, but there was a keen sense of alertness, ready for any signal of an instant departure.

They said I should get my things as soon as possible and plan to stay the night at the UNMISS base. Again, the Head of Security confidently stated that there would be gunfire that evening and if I did not hurry and organize myself, there would be no access later. He proudly stated that he did the same thing in Malakal during a previous uprising. He shut the gates and would not let anyone in when the fighting began. The staff member who accompanied Edward was sympathetic and said he would find a place with "AC" (air conditioning) for me to stay.

We were having difficulty believing what he had dogmatically said to us about what would happen that evening.

Maybe it was the peace that we had within ourselves and the presence of God with us in the face of the unknown. We trusted that God would show us what to do and had to live that way day by day. Why was this man so confident? What were the rebels saying to him? What was the government of South Sudan saying to him? There seemed to be something odd about this man's communication and his whole approach, but then what would I know as a novice and a foreign visitor? Not much, except that I have access to an interesting Sudanese network of people whose community fabric is knitted so tightly that it's almost waterproof. My connection to these people was growing. Sometimes I was frustrated by their lack of understanding of what I was trying to say and do, but equally, I was frustrated by my own lack of understanding of what they were saying and doing...but I digress.

We returned to the college compound in the late afternoon. Alex (the regional coordinator) dropped by. He said that people were beginning to panic and run away but there was no cause for alarm. The government would not let the rebels advance to Melut. "Nothing will happen." But was this confidence in the government's ability to respond misplaced? The ultimate target as mentioned earlier was the oil refinery near Paloich. The destruction of the last remaining oil refinery in South Sudan would mean the collapse of the country. The years of fighting for freedom would be for nought. They simply could not let that happen, but there was another factor to consider in terms of the army's ability to nip this rebel offensive in the bud.

Johnson Olony, an officer within the ranks of the SPLA had defected to the rebels. The army had entrusted him with a significant deployment of artillery to defend the northern reaches of South Sudan. Apparently, tanks, mortars and guns had now passed into the hands of the rebels. It was no longer gunfire alone. Now there was shelling whereby a whole village could be razed to the ground in a very short time, completely destroyed. It sounded to me that there were several tanks on the loose, equipped with the latest technology along with a barge with at least one large gun mounted on it, and most likely another barge carrying rebels and guns. They were probably already moving north to Melut at that very moment. I was told that the rebels had twenty-three tanks left (two recently destroyed by the SPLA), but I wondered about these numbers. Where were these tanks? Were some on the barges? How many could they carry on one barge? It sounded a lot to me. Possibly something was lost in translation. I read a report somewhere online about seven tanks but not twenty-three. Regardless, it was important to protect the oil refinery. The Dinka were trusting, or maybe hoping is a better word, that the government would regain control quickly.

Another question that arose in my mind was whether the SPLA still had the will to fight. When I turned on the television at night in Juba, CNN was repeatedly asking if the Iraqis had lost the will to fight in the Middle East. That was their latest revelation. I pondered how the SPLA'S confidence must have been shaken when Johnson Olony defected. Confusion, fear and panic could reign supreme for the local residents in an environment like this. The only hint of this was the sight of people walking by the roadside with a few belongings, or those who had walked to the UN base and waited patiently outside, hoping for shelter. There was no sense of panic. It was quiet except for a few UN and NGO vehicles moving around. Some of the people appeared to change their minds and return to their homes which were probably nearby in the town. It was surreal.

We tucked away that earlier piece of advice from Alex, the one about "nothing will happen". The conversation moved on to discuss dried soup mix and how to feed the displaced children and others. The organization that provided the soup mix was comprised of volunteers who glean vegetables from local farms in British Columbia. They dry a variety of vegetables, package them and send them for export with NGO's to overseas destinations. I was impressed with their professionalism and their dedication. I didn't want to let them down and hoped to give them a good report of how their labours had benefited and blessed people. One bag of soup mix made 100 cups of nutritious vegetable soup. However, it needed to be soaked for hours before cooking and for the quantity we needed to cook at the IDP camp, this could be challenging. We disagreed about the cooking time and process, so I gave our guest a bag of soup mix to work out how we could cook the contents the easiest way in the shortest amount of time, given that equipment was very limited. We had hoped to provide a meal the next day but it was too late to organize it now.

It seemed strange to be having a conversation about cooking soup mix after discussing the possibility of rebels coming to town. After I had packed a few essential items at the compound, we drove the short distance to the UN base. I was curious to stay there for a night anyway, but still had no sense of impending danger, only the knowledge that the rebels were planning to head this way. The unknown part was what the SPLA was doing at this time. What was the government doing to respond at this moment? I was led to the same area where we met the head of security earlier that afternoon. It was a courtyard bordered on three sides by three sets of sleeping quarters which looked like shipping containers. A major of the peacekeeping forces was present. With a European accent, he said to the Head of Security, "I would like to see the government do more." There seemed to be a delay in the response of the SPLA to the situation that was developing on the Nile River. However, there were many battles to fight concurrently in South Sudan and it was not known (at least not to me) where all the troops were deployed throughout the country at that time.

An administration officer wanted to charge me USD 42 for the night. This was for a bed and mattress in a demountable steel cabin. They informed me of this after having all but commanded me to stay at the base and then asked, "is that okay?" I said, "No, not okay. You should have told me this earlier." They finally relented and said, "Okay, just for one night you can stay, but you must get an emergency tent tomorrow to stay here at no charge." An emergency tent? From where? People were beginning to panic and flee. NGO's were either leaving or setting up their tents at the base. Local Sudanese were lining up at the gates hoping to get in. There was no sign of the rebels but something was in the air. I had no sense of panic. It was not yet time to go. If the rebels made it past Akoka, that would be the time to leave. I could not believe that I came all this way to evacuate and abandon a mission. I was not prepared to let go yet, but I knew that I had to swim with the tide.

I must say that I was glad of the possibility of a cool place to sleep and a real shower. My few nights in Melut so far had been sweat-soaked and relatively sleepless, maybe drifting off for 2 hours at a time and then waking to the sound of the birds singing in the trees the next day. The day before, I noticed a very striking small bird perched on the tap outside with the most brilliant red feathers contrasting with jet black. It was exquisite. I couldn't stop looking at it. As I reached for the cellphone, it darted off and I never saw it again. Then I noticed the butterflies. There was life in this place seemingly unhindered by the presence of mankind. A gecko had appeared on the old rickety, rusty fly screen on the window. I dared not touch the screen lest it fall apart.

The gecko looked well fed. The metal covers inside the window could be closed so I shut them each night for a feeling of privacy and a measure of apparent security even if it wasn't real.

At the UNMISS base, the promise of an air conditioner was soon fulfilled as I opened the door to the unit that provided sleeping quarters for two people. There were two basic single beds with used mattresses and an old air conditioner embedded in the wall. It had seen better days but looked like it might still work. I headed to the amenities block toward the back of the base. The Head of Security had commented that these facilities were never designed to service "all these people" (I guess the NGO's) who wanted to come and stay here. They were not maintained. Take them as you find them. I had no sheets nor pillow so I improvised. The air conditioner worked, but every ten minutes it would make a loud bang and wake me up so I shut it down. So glad I didn't pay USD 42 for that.

7
Plan B

The next morning, May 19, our driver was meant to arrive at 6.30 am. He didn't appear for another hour. He had been moving people out of the displaced people camp. Even the displaced people were being displaced. How does one live like that? How does one find food and water each day for a family?

Chagai already had a plan of what to do: "We will go to the airport for a security update." We returned to the compound where I gathered most of the remaining personal items. I left some Bible school materials and a DVD on the small table in the corner along with the bag of rice and other items we had bought three days before. The bar fridge was still full of containers of boiled rice left over from Achol's enthusiastic cooking on Saturday. This was not the time to clean the fridge so it stayed as is. I locked the two suitcases of humanitarian supplies and children's program resources believing that we would return within a week and continue our work. We had already agreed a date for going into the IDP camp and feeding children (and their families if possible). The suitcases were clearly labelled with yellow duct tape. We placed a large padlock on the compound door and left. The driver made one more stop for Chagai to collect his bag from a house further along the road. I began to feel anxious as we seemed to be heading in the wrong direction, but soon the driver turned around and headed for Paloich, which was about an hour away.

As we drove along, I saw a woman leading an elderly blind woman by a long stick to a place in a compound, supposedly to find a safe place for her to hide. Other women

41

piled their belongings on their heads and walked along the road away from Melut with family in tow. On the right-hand side, I saw 3 young children walking along seemingly in the middle of nowhere. It looked like an older sister about nine years of age with two younger siblings under seven years of age. What about them? I asked "What has happened to these children? Have they been abandoned by their parents?" At first Chagai said, "yes" but then added "or, they may belong to the village close by". As I turned toward the road ahead, I could see a village by the roadside. Yes, most likely the children were simply walking home. The urge to rescue people stirred simply out of what my eyes could see. What should we do? Nothing. Keep heading to the airport and wait for the next step. This is God's mission. He is leading. Don't be impulsive. Don't turn to the left or to the right. Wait.

I sat and waited with Adau, one of our volunteers, in the airport lounge. Expatriates were seated nearby waiting for their flights. This was probably the entire population of remaining foreign workers preparing to evacuate once again, upon hearing reports of rebel activity in the area. Adau disappeared talking on her cellphone. Chagai appeared mid-morning with an officer from airport security who gave this advice: "Right now, as you can see, there are still a few planes available. If you do not take one of these now, the military may take over the airport. In that case, civilians would no longer be able to fly. If you don't leave now, don't blame us if you are stuck here." The staff member left. That was pretty clear.

Chagai by now had heard that a Shilluk woman was saying "Let the people go." In other words, don't discourage them from leaving. Tell them to go." The Commissioner for Melut County who had been telling his people not to panic was now saying "yes, they should go." It was definitely time to leave. The latest news to reach Chagai was that a battle was taking place on the Nile River between two barges at that very moment and the potential outcome was anyone's guess. Army personnel were beginning to gather at the airport.

Being an eternal optimist, I still believed that all would be okay and the rebels would be defeated. But then I thought about the war that broke out in Juba in 2013 after my last visit. The battle moved up to Bor, north of Juba and then eventually reached Malakal. A massacre took place there in 2014. This was so difficult to accept. We never thought Malakal would be taken. Insecurity had now set in indefinitely thanks to the persistent supply of weapons to those bent on dividing and conquering. I pondered a "what if" scenario of returning to Melut soon and doing something useful.

My host managed to organize a ticket on a fully booked flight for me to Juba. (I discovered later that someone else was bumped from this flight. Most likely airport security or an airline manager gave me preference as a foreigner with an NGO over perhaps a Sudanese civilian or a soldier, but I will never know for sure.) Pastor Jack had apparently been trying to contact Chagai saying "get Helen out!". The timing was right. God is good.

Chagai rushed around looking for airport staff to process my baggage. There was no-one to be found. Finally, someone took the bag and managed to load it onto the right plane. It was probably the last one taken on board. I was hurried into the departure area. Everyone was calm, quiet and serious. After a while, I saw Chagai waving his arms at the door. I noticed Karen standing next to him. The security guard allowed me to leave the departure area and talk to her. She came to say goodbye. Her team were at the UN base very early that morning when I was waiting to depart. I did not realize they were coming to Paloich also. We shared our disappointments about having to evacuate and wanting to stay on at Melut. I recall her saying that we cannot be presumptuous in these situations. She was right. I witnessed to that. Unless God clearly directs one to stay, evacuation is the prudent thing. The work could wait. We said our goodbyes and hoped our paths would cross again. Karen was hoping that although they would temporarily relocate to another field office, they would all return to Melut very soon. She left and I hurried back inside.

My water bottle was empty. I was thirsty and there was no sign of a vending machine or store. There was nothing at Paloich airport. It was a skeletal place; only seats to wait on and bare walls to survey. I noticed three Sudanese gentlemen dressed in military attire with some colourful braiding and adornments indicating senior ranking of some kind. They were possibly SPLA but not necessarily. The police, military and UN uniforms were beginning to look the same to me. I forgot which was which. I was not sure how much longer I would have to wait before I could get some water. What should I do? The three men were seated together in a huddle. There were several large unfinished bottles of water on their table along with an array of used cups. It looked like several people had attended a meeting and they were the three remaining participants.

Did I have the courage to ask for some water? They had what I needed and it seemed like it would go to waste anyway. I stepped towards them. At the sound of "excuse me", all three gentlemen looked up and stopped talking. The one who appeared to be leading the discussion frowned at me for interrupting (although they did seem to notice me approaching them a moment before.)

"Would you have some water to spare? I have run out. I wondered if you would mind if I take some," I asked. He leaned forward and took hold of a bottle that was half full, but another officer smiled at me and handed me a full bottle.

He said, "No-one has drunk from this bottle. Don't worry." I thanked them and returned to the line that had formed for boarding the plane. I could have made it without the bottle of water, but it did no harm to ask. The men resumed their discussion as if nothing had happened.

By 12:30, my plane left. It was most likely a company charter plane. There was no recognizable logo. A flight attendant with a South African accent firmly directed passengers. Chagai and Adau were able to take a cargo flight around the same time with wounded soldiers, but there was no air conditioning and it was extremely hot, odorous and unpleasant. I wondered about this privilege that I had of flying in comfort while others flew by cargo, but I rested in the knowledge that God organized it and there were no options here. I needed to simply go with the protocol laid out before me.

We returned safely to Juba without incident. There was no room at the Heaven Hotel, so I moved into the hotel opposite. I had stayed here on my initial visit to South Sudan. A young man who worked there seemed familiar. We vaguely remembered each other. In the course of conversation, he informed me that he needed to take his sister to the hospital for an injection for typhoid. I offered to pray for her if he could bring her to the hotel. He seemed keen to do that.

Chagai and Pastor Jack sat in the courtyard glued to their cellphones monitoring events in the Upper Nile. We heard that the rebels defeated the SPLA on the river. However, reinforcements were sent in so the rebels should be driven back in the next day or so. The SPLA then sank one of the 2 rebel boats on the river. Anything could happen. We remained hopeful of returning to Melut.

The next morning, May 20, Chagai came. The Heaven Hotel room 114 was available if I wanted it. I wondered if it was worth moving, but decided I would as it was still before the 11.00 am checkout time. I packed my bags and noticed that the combination lock appeared to have been tampered with. I wondered if that was the work of one of the hotel staff or if I simply had not noticed this earlier. I was glad to move just in case.

Across the road, I settled back into my room. Chagai and I sat in the central courtyard. He informed me that the rebels had attacked Melut at 7.00pm on the previous night. That meant that we had departed the region only 6.5 hours before. This was a sobering thought, but it pointed to God's quiet and sure way of guiding us out of a dangerous situation. He was in control and his timing was perfect. It was like a parent gently guiding a toddler away from something that could hurt them, shielding them from knowing how big and scary that thing really was.

We were aware that many people had fled into the bush between Melut and Paloich. They would soon need water and food and their cellphone batteries would soon die. James Chagai was out there somewhere. He was heading for Paloich on foot. I wondered what we could do for these people.

After pondering options, I contacted the local International Red Cross and advised them of the situation. They empathized. Unfortunately, they had similar situations to deal with on many fronts. They listened and acknowledged the need to organize a response but could not do it for a few days. However, they were interested to interview the people to pinpoint their location and determine their immediate needs such as medical help, water, and so on. We agreed to contact those who had fled and to ask permission to give out their cell numbers to the IRC. Sadly, we were no longer able to connect with the people in the bush by phone.

Meanwhile, the situation in Melut was grave. Rebels apparently had burned down the town. Fighting continued.

At some point during the day, I received a phone call from the young man whose sister had typhoid. They were ready for me to pray. I went across the street and joined them. I didn't think that people with typhoid simply walked around the streets like this. I thought they laid in hospital beds.

When I visited Malakal Hospital in 2013, I saw a woman lying in bed with a group of people gathered around her. The nurse advised that this patient had typhoid and one other illness. I think it might have been malaria. The doctor spent between five and ten minutes trying to find a vein to inject the woman. She was elderly. Her skin was paper thin stretched over her bones. There did not seem to be much hope. The volunteer with me said that we should move on, but I hung on hoping for an opportunity to pray for the woman. Again, I was advised to move on, but I dug in and insisted on being able to pray briefly. I touched the tips of the woman's fingers and prayed for her life. We left quickly and as we stepped outside of the hospital doors onto a path, an eerie scream erupted from those still gathered around the woman's bed. She had breathed her last. It was almost like she was on a trajectory to a very dark place. It was frightening. Surreal.

I recall thinking "Oh no! I pray for a sick person and she immediately dies. The relatives might blame me for her death. Let's get out of here. Who knows what tribal law might come into play." I was familiar with the tribally enforced "payback" system of Papua New Guinea. I had seen it in action and can recall the kind of event such as a motor vehicle accident whereby an expatriate had to leave on the next plane home because a national resident had been killed or injured.

8
Mission Possible: Juba

On May 21st, Chagai and I talked at 8.30 am about a few operational matters that needed to be changed. There was tension over payment of the person driving, refuelling costs, people tagging along and leadership decisions that needed to be made. We moved on to discuss a plan for Juba to reconfigure the mission so that we could still accomplish what we set out to do assuming this was God's plan. This was better. We agreed to go out to a place called "New Site" and spend some time with the children there. First, we went to the market in Juba town and bought a football, a volleyball, two plastic balls, a flip chart, marker pens, and chalk.

About mid-afternoon we headed out to a throng of children singing and playing drums in a mud and bamboo church with a nice sturdy timber "A" frame covered by a tin roof. I talked to the children, showed them how to make the sound of rain and storms with their hands and feet, sang songs and then taught them to play some competitive ball-games.

The competition was fierce between the boys and the girls. The will to win was pulsing through the room. The games were close, bringing screams and squeals when balls were dropped or misdirected. I noticed some shuffling of team members. A young girl aged about 11 ran out of the room in tears. I said, "She is part of the team and should stay on the team," but the girls were serious about winning. "She doesn't know how to play!" they said firmly. It was survival of the fittest, but I countered with "she is learning just as you are." I went after the girl and persuaded her to return.

49

After the excitement of several competitions, we ended the games. A few of us sat in the shade outside of the building. Chagai introduced a young woman to me. She was wearing a prosthetic limb. Her leg had been blown off by a landmine (but I was not sure when) and her husband was killed in December 2014 during the civil war. I saw several people around Juba who were missing legs. I met a man on crutches named Victor outside of the hotel one day. A land-mine took his leg 7 years earlier in Juba. He was a follower of Jesus in the humblest of circumstances. Victor was glad to receive prayer. I cannot imagine how one lives day to day in that situation but with Christ, all things are possible and God is taking care of him.

Back at the hotel, I went through the comical routine of trying to order a meal from the Eritrean cook who could not speak English. She would grab Ali whose English was passable to translate between the two of us. I would say "I would like some spaghetti for dinner please." Ali would turn to me and say, "you want spaghetti?" I would say "yes, spaghetti".

He would ask "spaghetti? No meat?"

I would answer "yes, I want meat."

Ali would ask "you want spaghetti with meat?"

I would answer "yes, spaghetti with meat."

He would turn to the cook and explain it to her.

She would say something.

He would ask me again "you want spaghetti, with meat on top?"

"Yes", I said, "Spaghetti with meat on top."

We went through this almost daily. Confirming, reconfirming.

Finally, an enormous plate of spaghetti with meat on top would arrive at my door. The plate was always filled with as much pasta as could possibly fit on one dinner plate. I would eat as much of it as I could and when I returned the unfinished meal to the staff, they were worried.

Ali would ask "why didn't you eat all of it?" I tried to explain that I was very full and ate as much as I possibly could. It was an enormous serving. It really could feed at least two people but no matter how I tried to explain this to the cook, the plate was consistently the biggest plate of pasta that one could possibly serve.

Language was challenging. Every day I felt frustrated by the miscommunications and misunderstandings over the smallest things as well as over ministry and process. But God showed us the humour of it also.

One day, I was in the hotel office talking to Ali. Pastor Jack came by, stood outside of the office doorway, and said, "I am coming".

I said, "You are coming?"

"Yes", he said, "I am coming".

I said, "You mean, you are coming now from somewhere, or you are going, then you are coming back."

He said "Yes, I am going, then I am coming."

"Oh", I said, "You are coming after you are going."

We all burst out laughing at the absurdity of the conversation.

From that day on, Ali and I had an "in" joke about whether we were going or coming on any given day. Finally, there was a place of connection between our cultures where we "got it". We all saw the humour of the situation at the same time. This was a precious moment. This was a moment of pure joy, a taste of heaven. We all felt the lightness and the hilarity of it there at the Heaven Hotel.

I woke up on May 22nd, feeling condemned, depressed, and out of alignment with everything. I looked at my workshop papers and felt confused about what to do next. I needed to get out of the hotel room which was now quite dark as the lights went out at 7.00 am. I needed a different space.

There was a bar adjacent to the courtyard so I thought "perhaps I could sit in a corner and use it like an office for the morning". No-one would be there at this hour. I began to read the work of Roy Clements who wrote about the early Christian church. Some of the female staff gathered for a meal of Injira. This consisted of a large rice pancake laid on a large round tray. Two different kinds of topping were tipped onto the rice bread. There was a meat dish with garlic and onion, and also a chickpea, garlic, tomato and onion concoction.

The women urged me to join them and eat with them, so I did. I asked how they felt about living in Juba. They said they were always afraid. One of these women literally wets her pants at the sound of gunfire. She had been traumatized. The Ethiopian woman said, "It is not guns we fear. It is rape. You can shoot me. I don't care... but it is rape that we are afraid of. The first thing the soldiers do is rape the women. I asked why she thinks they do that. She said, "I don't know. Maybe they don't really know what they are fighting for. They are just people of violence."

I offered to pray for the traumatized woman and then extended it to the whole group of four. So we had a healing prayer session in the bar that morning. I invited them to bring their friends for prayer too.

It had been mentioned that I could preach on Sunday at church. I wondered if I had time to write a message. There was no particular message on my mind. God did not seem to give specific direction on this so I left it for now. I went to the internet café trying to find Wi-Fi for the IPAD to deal with storage issues but did not succeed. I decided to have a cup of ice cream on the way home. That was lunch. I would have a meal at the end of the day. How providential that there should be a shop with a soft serve ice cream machine in a place like Juba...and it was only across the road. It might be the only one in South Sudan.

I began to write out a schedule for the evangelism workshop and reviewed my notes. By about 3.00 pm I had finished. Pastor Jack and Chagai arrived at 4.10 pm. We headed out to New Site to meet with the leaders. The children excitedly ran to meet us. There was no sign of the leaders so I taught the children how to play a new game called "captain ball". Afterwards, they went outside to play football and volleyball of sorts. Leaders of the church arrived in the meantime. We discussed our proposal for the evangelism workshop and the children's program and the provision of food. They seemed agreeable to these ideas. On Sunday morning, I shared our plans at their church service and prayed for the congregation and their country.

Chagai heard from James Chagai. He was in the Paloich area and he was okay. We continued to hope that we could go back to Melut again, but the rebels were still fighting near Akoka. They would not give up. I guess they were too close to their target now to do that. The SPLA apparently had recaptured another four tanks which was encouraging...only nineteen to go...if Chagai's earlier report of about twenty-four tanks in total was accurate. I still thought that figure sounded too high. Perhaps it was more like 7 tanks, less 4 leaves 3 tanks on the loose? Who knows?

The next morning, May 23, the request for breakfast went through the same translation procedure. Even though my request was the same each time, the cook would look anxious and would ask Ali to tell her what it is that I wanted her to cook. The safe choices were basically omelette or scrambled egg. In fact, they were probably the only choices. I always said "omelette" in the hope that the cook would instantly know what I meant after the first few days. However, she started adding bread rolls which complicated things. I tried to explain that she could leave out the bread rolls, but this only led to a different kind of bread roll, no matter how many versions of "no" I gave with the shaking of the head, hand movements, and body language. I was also receiving two bread rolls now so it seemed that she was being generous in the hope that I would be happy so I thanked her for her delicious omelette. It was not your usual omelette. It was a kind of scrambled egg omelette, chopped up with onion and green pepper and was quite tasty.

I noticed an African hotel guest criticizing the way his chicken was cooked one evening. He was expecting four-star quality from a two-star place and from a young woman who was possibly employed by her friends with no formal training. Jobs were scarce in South Sudan. These conversations took place in the courtyard for all to see and hear. It was something akin to a soap opera unfolding each day.

I met a Sudanese engineer who sat nearby with his laptop. Apparently, his family were refugees in the United States, which began to raise questions in my mind. Best to leave some things alone. There seem to be many fathers working and living in countries separate from their families these days. The soap opera also included a soldier who would sit in the courtyard facing the gate with what may have been a machine gun by his side, waiting for a driver to collect him. That's a whole other character waiting to be developed.

I made coffee in my room with the help of Ali each day. He suggested I buy milk powder from a store which I did yesterday along with a small jar of Nescafé. I originally brought a cheap container of Maxwell House instant coffee from Canada, but it was left behind in Melut. The taste of instant coffee was of course distinctly different from freshly ground coffee. However, to have coffee at all and a cup of hot water delivered to my room (no charge) was a treat and a blessing for which I was thankful.

I spent some time working on my workshop notes in the courtyard. Any opportunity to do that is a gift. At some point, I received an update on Melut. The latest news was that the rebels were now at Kodok and may go back over the border into Sudan. We were also advised that people had run to the UNMISS base at Melut when the gunfire began a few days ago but were locked out. Men, women and children are believed to have been shot and killed at the gates. Their bodies remained there for several days from what we understand. The SPLA apparently began to occupy the area. I was informed that it would take at least one week for them to give clearance to civilians for occupation. Bodies had to be removed, possibly by burning or throwing them into the river. Hopes of returning to Melut were beginning to fade fast. The fact was that even if we had access, people had fled, there would most likely be no food nor water, and no transport. Forget it. Not going to happen. Let it go.

Pastor Jack arrived at 2.20 pm. He had offered to take me with him for a visit to the IDP camp. First, he collected his brother from the airport and drove him home. Finally, we made it to the camp and met with families who had recently arrived from the north. In one area, people were issued with blue tents as shelter. Several families would live in one tent. In another area, IDP's were like squatters living in abandoned houses. If the owner returned, they simply moved on to the next house. The families that we met all had to flee from somewhere at some time.

The last household that we visited was made up of many adults and children. They fled from Paloich the previous Wednesday with nothing. They had little food, and no cooking pots except for a few items borrowed. They were trusting God but it was so difficult. The oldest man there said they were very encouraged that someone would come to see them when others would not come. I felt so sorry for their situation. I wanted to give them something. The needs that I became aware of daily were overwhelming. I pondered a list of items that I had recorded in my notebook to mull over. It included hiring a bus to take IDPs to the Ugandan border, where they could at least have food and water and perhaps medical care at a UN refugee camp.

That evening, I called one of the IRC (Red Cross) field coordinators to give them two reference points for displaced people in the bush. Apparently, there were some old wells in the area that may or may not have water. Their staff had been diligent to contact me a few times for information. I was impressed with how accessible they were and how professional, efficient and compassionate, all at the same time.

I bought a one litre container of mango nectar from the bar and took it to my room. There was no refrigerator so I could not save half for the next day. It felt excessive to drink it all at once, but it was either that or tip it down the sink. It tasted so good chilled, and was the only fruit I had so I finished it during the course of the evening. It was imported from Egypt.

For dinner, I ate a protein bar from Canada. I was out of water again, so I headed down to the bar to buy 3 more bottles. I dared not go to bed without having drinkable water in the room. There would be no chance before about 8.00 am the next day to restock. There were days when bottled water became scarce around Juba depending which part of town you visited. I carried a water filter with me but relied on bottled water while it was available for safety and convenience. For a longer-term visit, I would like to use more sustainable practices.

Karen, the nurse that I stayed with in Melut sent an email on May 23rd. The day her team landed in their next field office, the UN feared the airstrip might be taken over by the government, so they evacuated to Kenya. It was so disappointing for all of them. The house next to hers had been totally looted. The local caretaker said that he tried to fend off the thieves but his life was threatened.

9
Take A Walk on The New Side

I prepared a message for the church at New Site for Sunday morning regarding Jesus as repairer of broken walls from Isaiah 61:1-4. It went something like this: "The enemy has broken down the walls of your heart – brought fear. He has tried to traumatize you. He wants to destroy those who belong to the Lord (Revelation 12:17). Jesus has come to destroy the works of the devil (1 John 3:8). He comes to bind up the broken hearted. You should not be paralyzed by fear and without peace." We prayed for healing for the people at church and for the nation of South Sudan.

I did not realize that the commissioner for Baliet County, James Torr was present until he stood up to speak. He asked the congregation to make a special offering for the displaced people of the Paloich area who had to flee from Melut. I liked his leadership.

I set up the projector and laptop after church, but there was a cable missing to connect with the sound system. I had asked previously if all the cables were available and was told "yes" and not to worry. This was the beginning of a journey of frustration. I asked questions ahead of time on several occasions so that we would not have to make two trips or spend an afternoon looking through a market for something at the last minute. But no matter what I did, something was always missing. I pondered this. Was it the translation of English to Sudanese that was not working? At times, the Sudanese gave the impression that they knew exactly what I was talking about, but in practice, they did not. I most likely had to learn a local language to solve this.

The leader of the church was waiting for us to give them money to purchase food for the evangelism workshop which would begin the next morning. This was our understanding. However, when Chagai arrived for the meeting, the leader said we should go now to the market with a volunteer from the church. This did not sit well with me, but it seemed like we had no choice. I should have said, "no, not possible today". It could have been done early the following day. I see Sunday as a day of rest and a time when we simply stop and re-create. We don't do shopping that can wait another day. When I run out of gas on a Sunday, of course I refill the car, but I could have refilled the car the day before. It takes a shift of mindset to be proactive and to prepare for a day of rest. I believe it pleases God when we honour the idea of resting from our usual labours as He did. It is part of a lifestyle that is submitted and surrendered to Him. I felt robbed of my rest this day and the whole market expedition turned out to be a fiasco.

The storekeepers increased their prices because they saw a white woman present. The Sudanese with me began to argue with them. I trusted my Sudanese companions to know how to handle their own purchasing and dealing with their local traders, but from my observation, they were agreeing to prices that were too high. We began to make offers until the merchant understood that we were not willing to pay his top price. The volunteer from the church selected a set of trays that were not on our shopping list. I found out later that the leaders had told him what they wanted. I was bothered by this at first, but later allowed a few of these items to be included. I had to remember that the church literally had nothing, except for one large glass mug for drinking water. Later, I observed how the trays were used by the women serving tea repeatedly. That was a good call after all. It was challenging making decisions about money on the spot in front of everyone. They could not possibly know what was going through my mind at that moment. I knew almost every figure in the budget because I had been over it so many times. I had cast and recast the figures. The final figure had to be low enough to gain sufficient support for the mission to go ahead. I knew this was God's mission. It had to be accomplished. No self-respecting project manager would settle for anything less.

A storm was coming. The storekeeper began to rush us as he wanted to close his store. We were spending quite an amount of money with him, but he rudely took the cash and waved us out onto the street. He could care less. Chagai and I were upset by this attitude and made mental notes about whom to avoid next time. We went across the way to another store to buy large tins of milk powder. They were charging what seemed excessive amounts. Once more the Sudanese began to exchange words with the storekeeper. One of our team threw his arms in the air and expressed his disgust at how things were going. "To be honest, I will never do this again!" he said (but he did). The whole event was almost comical. We settled on a figure in another store. This became our benchmark. We learned the prices quickly and toward the end of the mission, the storekeepers learned to treat us very well and give us reasonable prices. We also devised a purchasing strategy of sending in the Sudanese to get quotes on some items, while I stayed with the driver. On our last visit to the market, I walked into a store, named the price that I thought was reasonable for a can of milk powder and the deal was done with a smile.

When we returned to the hotel, I noticed that the Sudanese had spoken exclusively in their language all day and barely included me in their conversations. I must say that I noticed the same thing in Vancouver. When someone who could barely speak English was sitting at the table, we often tended to speak as if they were not there. The person almost becomes invisible. I felt alienated. I cried tears of frustration this night. Something had changed. There was a shift in the atmosphere. I needed to step back and see what was happening. There was clearly an outside influence moving in.

We were moving into a tough place and were poised to teach an evangelism workshop. Many NGO's had withdrawn staff from Juba and here we were about to implement a mission that we believed God was behind. And He was. I remembered... *"If you can take it, you can make it!"* We were going to make it, no matter how frustrating, no matter how misunderstood I felt each day, no matter what it would take at the market to buy what we needed, no matter how many times I had to ask, "can someone please start the generator!". Even when Pastor Jack purchased fuel that day, the gas station attendant withheld some of the change. Pastor Jack was unable to get any sense out of the situation, so he asked me to talk to the attendant. I went over and began to go over step by step carefully with the attendant the price of the gas, what I gave him etc. Everyone gathered around and listened. He was fuelling someone else's car while I talked to him. He shook his head and was adamant that he had given me the right change.

I wondered what this scenario looked like to the local people. Did I look like a bossy foreigner throwing my weight around and brow beating a poor local, or, was this a reasonable exchange that was based on telling the truth? I allowed the local people to judge. Perhaps though there was something else going on for this young man. We had no idea of how Westerners may have treated him in the past and perhaps he simply closed his ears even though what I was saying was quite true. Perhaps he made a mistake and now had to save face in front of the men standing around. Perhaps he was incredibly busy and simply forgot what I had given him.

When gas was available, vehicles would line up down the street and wait for quite a while to buy fuel. Motor cycle riders would form a long line and when they were close to the bowser, they would gather three or four bikes and move the nozzle from one tank to the other. There seemed to be only one attendant with no break. One day, at a different gas station, I counted about 90 vehicles waiting. Whatever the reason, it was time to move on.

10
Finally, A Workshop!

For the next three days, May 25 to 27, we ran an evangelism workshop at New Site Church. This church had been planted in a place where army soldiers lived along with some displaced people. Many of the soldiers had relatives who fled fighting and came to live with them. Some of the workshop attendees lived here, some came from a church across town, and others came from a church even further out.

While driving to New Site on the first day, Pastor Jack hit a dog. I still feel the pain of seeing that dog running across the road yelping. It was heart wrenching. Who would take care of it? Pastor Jack continued as if nothing happened. Different culture. I closed my eyes. "Lord, please heal the dog!" We were almost there when I realized that I needed water. We called into a gas station, but there was no water for sale. I bought some biscuits and we drove on to the church. It had rained heavily the night before. One woman was there at 8.45 am. A few others trickled in. The church was asking for money for water. We had tried to arrange these things a few days earlier and still nothing was organized. We had to start from scratch with logistics. Finally, someone went to buy drinking water for the workshop participants and cooking water for the cooks.

We started the workshop around 10.45 am. The people were patient. I still had no water. Neither did they. My mouth was so dry. Chagai went on a mission (on the back of a motor bike taxi) and finally arrived with three or four bottles of water for me, but then I did not want to drink it in front of the Sudanese people. I forgot about the water and pressed on. I found that I survived along with everyone else.

65

Eventually, the large jerry can of drinking water came, but no-one rushed for it. These people had endured thirst and hunger. Most of them were very thankful to God that they were still alive. It seemed like they have been through the school of patient endurance.

It took a while, but finally a cup of tea came at 1.00 pm much to the relief of the attendees. A meal was served at 4.00 pm. Several of the youth and a few pastors were in attendance. We had about 72 signed up by the end of the day. That included some of the ladies who cooked. The food looked very good. Everyone seemed to be enjoying it. People persistently shoved plates in my direction, concerned that I had not eaten. I finally took some food and ate. Later, I found the men drinking tea outside in the shade, so I joined them. I loved the way every person present greeted you with a handshake and an acknowledgement. Even the youth would come by and shake the hand of every person present, even if they only came to talk to one person. Everyone was included. They seemed to think and act collectively. They really lived like family.

We reached the hotel around 5.30 pm. I felt stretched by the constant logistical challenges and was mindful that I needed to muzzle my mouth in case those useless words of frustration should fly out. I preached to myself "Do not complain." I tried my best to ebb and flow with what would happen each day, knowing that this was the best way. Until December 2014, I had been working with an engineering project team where professional meetings, scheduling and logistics were the order of the day on a major project. God had released me from that and transplanted me into a world where time was not the master of all things. In fact, the schedule was now a poor attempt to get control of what He, the Great Architect of the universe was doing. I began to let go of the need to chide the driver for being late (even quietly in my mind). It was the Holy Spirit who had arranged the timing of everything. He was incorporating all the elements of the day into a symphony, a rhythm that was beyond anything that man could orchestrate. For this we gave thanks.

Each morning, I led a short session of healing prayer to minister to the needs of the traumatized. Everyone in the room had experienced the loss of someone during the war or had witnessed violence. No-one escaped the terror of this and the psychological scarring. One morning, I asked those who had recurring bad dreams to raise their hands. Only one woman raised her hand, then two. I invited them to come forward for prayer. Another three people joined them at the front. We prayed for deliverance from trauma and for peace for their minds.

We ploughed through a basic theological understanding of what evangelism is, what an evangelist is, and what our responsibility as believers is, with reflections from both a seasoned, published evangelist, John Dickson and Dr J.I. Packer, an internationally respected theologian who has a very straight approach to expressing his ideas. As C.S. Lewis taught "say what you mean, mean what you say." We also looked at the journey of conversion and the experience of the early church up to about the 5th century. We talked about Christendom and the impact on the church and the remnants that we see of that today.

One aspect of this discussion that stood out was infant baptism. We noted the law that Emperor Justinian passed in 529 AD, requiring that all infants must be baptized. The fact that this did not come out of a theological place, but out of a Roman law was an important fact for people to know. It should have driven all of us back to Scripture to see what Jesus did and what Jesus said, especially regarding the Great Commission (Matthew 28:18-20). The pastors did not say anything and I have no idea what discussion may have taken place back in their own churches. I wondered if I might be called to explain myself, having raised a foundational theological issue that would challenge some, but nothing happened.

I liked to facilitate group work to promote discussion, thought, connections between the participants and feedback. The Sudanese were very thoughtful about the discussion questions and liked to present a full picture when they reported on behalf of their groups. The group numbering was important to them. They tended to number themselves and I needed to make sure I called on them in order. All their key points were recorded on the flip chart. We would then tally the results, and summarize the overall position. On this occasion, each of the 5 groups were asked to present their top 5 challenges for evangelism in their local context. The issues they raised (beginning with the most commonly cited) were as follows:

1. Security - Fighting/war is ongoing; tribalism is closely related to security.
2. Training - Lack of training in evangelism.
3. Faith - Lack of faith, meaning that people do not want to believe in God.
4. Materials - Lack of materials, including Bibles.
5. Prayer - Don't know how to pray; can't evangelize people without prayer.
6. Food - Lack of food.
7. Transport - Lack of transport.
8. Displacement.

It was clear that the violence and ongoing fighting in South Sudan was blocking everything good. It prevented every positive work for the nation. As long as the fighting could continue to be fuelled by those giving arms to the rebels, South Sudan could never move forward. However, some of the local people were willing to go out and evangelize if someone would support them to do so. They needed the cost of transportation to be paid. They needed Bibles.

One man showed me his well-worn set of colored pictures that he uses for sharing the gospel one on one. From what I understood, he wanted a replacement for these plus some more evangelism resources. A volunteer was keen to say "oh, tell Helen how many you want and she will organize them for you." I quickly said, "No, let me see what we can do." I noted these requests for when I could assess the funds available and the priorities. We needed to listen carefully for requests for ministry resources as these people were willing to serve the Lord in their communities. I don't think I listened well enough to the details, but I didn't forget the man nor his request.

There were a few opportunities for people to share during the workshop. One woman stood up and talked about her lack of hope. Her husband died during the war. She had to flee from the fighting in Malakal. Many were killed there so she was blessed to be alive still. However, she had no hope in Juba. She was traumatized by the violence and the uprooting of her life and the loss and grief of it all. We prayed as a large group later that day and included a prayer for the Lord to restore hope for her. By the end of the day, she was beaming. The Lord had quietly done something special for her. She repeatedly came to me over the next day, shaking my hand and smiling. This is what the Lord wanted to do for his people in Juba. Beauty for ashes. This was the power of encouragement.

As in 2013, there was a strong message for the Western church – a Macedonian cry. The people shared these concerns for the church in South Sudan:

1. Lack of pastors/Pastors are leaving churches to work for the government;
2. Islam is spreading by targeting children and giving money to leaders all through South Sudan;
3. Need encouragement from the West for leaders and churches.

I always found it interesting and helpful to hear their assessment of the state of the church and of the nation. It was also wonderful to see a mixture of church leaders, women and youth in attendance sharing their views. I took advantage of the presence of the youth in the workshop to speak to them about praying "big" prayers to God (i.e. ask for God to do great things in and through their lives for their nation.) If they wanted to do great things for God, they needed to read their Bibles and pray and commit themselves wholeheartedly. I encouraged those who sensed a call to evangelism to pray about this. Perhaps the Lord would send them out to evangelize their people.

One of the leaders made a telling observation: "It was the United States who brought us the gospel, but where are they now? There are no missionaries." At a time when NGOs were pulling out their staff, the believers of South Sudan were asking for brothers and sisters in Christ to come and support them, teach them, train them and encourage them. Where were their brothers and sisters in Christ? Their understanding was that we were certainly able to come, but we chose not to. Should government travel advisories dictate the spread of the gospel? *Governments do not send missionaries. God does.* How many people have sung "Here am I, Lord...Send me" or a similar phrase on Sunday morning? I recall one of the SIM websites which listed a prayer request in 2013 for "fearless, godly people" to join them on the mission field in South Sudan. Seeing that prayer request reinforced my belief that God was calling me to go there.

The workshop ended on Wednesday and everyone went on their way. We provided assistance with transportation for a number of people as they had travelled quite a distance. A few of them had attended the first workshop in Malakal. I wondered how much had been achieved through this workshop. It was what the relief society requested. I pondered this. Well, the attendees had received Biblical input, read Scriptures together, they had eaten a solid, cooked meal and drank tea together, they received healing through prayer, they were encouraged and were built up in their faith. If all of that was true, then God had cared for His people. The best indicator though was probably Chagai's feedback. He said, "The people are happy, very happy." A leader from another church asked if the workshop could be repeated for them. We agreed to squeeze it into the two days prior to my departure.

11
Getting to Know the Neighbours

I worked at the hotel the next morning and prepared a shopping list for the children's program. It was a short walk to the local stationery shop, past the young men leaning on their motor bike taxis. I bought pens and exercise books for the youth leaders. The storekeeper gave me a free roller ball pen for being a "good customer" as I had been there several times. The pen disappeared the following week when I lent it to someone at the church. Easy come, easy go. Perhaps it was considered now to be a community pen?

Pastor Jack came about 2.30 pm to collect me. We attended to some errands including a trip to the Bible Society to look at their stock of Bibles in English and Dinka Padang. Mading, a friend of Pastor Jack's was there. He lived in Australia at the time and was visiting family in Juba. I can't remember what work he was doing in Australia, but the Sudanese who have been fortunate enough to have a university education are very proud of it. If only all of them could have this opportunity. The frequency of tribal conflicts would decrease markedly if the children and youth of this generation were to go to school. After visiting the people of Malakal, it seemed to me that given a chance, they would do more with their opportunities than many of us in the West, who have had an abundance of choices of education.

Pastor Jack was not well. He had malaria. He dropped me off and went home to lie down. I noticed a clinic nearby and dropped in to ask about clinic fees and malaria treatment. The staff immediately referred me to the doctor. I was surprised by the way this physician took me into his office and gave me about 15 minutes of his time. He seemed very happy to share about his patient care, diagnosis and treatment of malaria, consultation and lab test fees, drug purchasing policy, and the dangers of rogue pharmaceuticals etc. He seemed to be a conscientious medical professional who cared about his patients and loved what he did.

I decided to have a meal at the hotel across the road. Some of the staff there invited me to share a meal of Injira with them even though I had already ordered a meal of chicken and chips. They insisted "eat!", "eat!" several times so I gladly ate with them. It was wonderful once again to be included like family and what was even more surprising was how much younger they were than I. It was possibly the novelty of being the only white face in the neighbourhood but I was also a regular customer. Ultimately, I knew it was the Holy Spirit who set this up.

A young woman entered. She was tipsy. Drawing up a chair, she introduced herself as "Aker" (not her real name) and announced that she was a relative of the President. Aker was striking. Her ebony skin was stunning to me, almost perfect. My white skin was freckled and blotched with veins showing. How strange we must have appeared to the Sudanese. When Aker discovered what I was doing in South Sudan, she proceeded to challenge me about why I was not helping the people in Malakal. She said they are suffering badly. "You people from NGO's and churches...why are you not working there? I have helped these people out of my own pocket!"

A man with no shirt suddenly came to the window and announced "It's true! It's true!" There had been gunfire and fighting near or around Juba today. According to Aker, security personnel had already called to reassure her that the incident was over. Apparently, this man was confirming the fighting issue, but I was not sure what was really going on. Aker spoke very confidently. I was intrigued by all this. She said to come and visit them at their apartments nearby. I was glad of the open invitation.

Meanwhile, where was the meal I had ordered? My cheeken and cheaps? I think the cook forgot and may even have gone home. Perhaps he got wind of the rumour about unrest and gunfire and left. The young man in charge looked worried and disappeared. A while later, my meal appeared. I wondered who cooked it. Maybe the young man was embarrassed that I waited so long and took care of it himself. Either way, I finally ate my meal for the day and went back to the Heaven Hotel. I was thirsty and felt like drinking something other than water. I dropped into the bar and asked if they had a lemon drink and, joy of joys, one of the women produced a bottle of chilled bitter lemon soda which was heaven sent! You had to be there and feel the heat to appreciate how good this tasted. I looked at some incoming email and sent a couple out.

12

A Long Day

On Saturday, the youth were holding an event at the New Site church. On the way to the church that morning, we stopped at the IDP camp. New families were arriving every day in Juba. It was common for several families to share one tent. The camp was only meant to be a temporary shelter (as with all the other IDP camps), but the numbers were growing rapidly. I recall people standing around outside the tents. We met a few of the newcomers.

As we were leaving, a child walked toward me and said what sounded like "water". They were waiting for a truck to arrive and replenish their water tank. I did not know what to do. "If I give this one water, there are many others watching nearby who also want water." Wrong call. The lesson I learned in children's ministry years ago was to go with the one standing in front of you as most likely God has sent them for a reason. Don't worry about all the "what if's", just do it. I wish I had given him what I had. If there was one thing I would revisit and change, it would be this. I wanted to hire a water truck and solve the problem. The water trucks were funded by the government to supply the camp, but clearly it was an inadequate service. "Lord, please bring the water soon."

We were told the youth event would start at 10.00 am and probably finish around 2.00 pm, but when we arrived there were only a handful of people present. Transport was difficult and costly for them. One of the leaders asked us if we would show the Jesus film, but we didn't bring the necessary equipment. Around 11.30 am, we decided to drive to the Konyo Konyo market where we bought supplies for the next week's program and then collected the projector and laptop from the hotel. How convenient that the youth should schedule an event like this, two days before the children's program. This gave us a platform to recruit at least 30 young people to join our team.

Returning to the event around 1.30 pm, we found the meeting in full swing, with a large group of youth singing and dancing. The place was alive. The leader handed the microphone to me. I shared about the mission and the children's program for next week, inviting youth to join us for training on Monday. When I looked at their faces around the room, I saw such great potential for their nation. I said, "When I look at your faces, I see the future of South Sudan". Some of the young adults smiled and clapped their hands.

Although they asked us to show the Jesus film at 3.00 or 4.00 pm, they were still dancing and singing at 5:15 pm. Time meant nothing. I don't recall hearing any repetition in their repertoire of songs either. They had such a great sense of community. About ten of them would gather at the front to lead all at once. Apparently, you could sing in the choir if you could squeeze into the space in front of the pulpit. At 5.25 pm, they finally opened the Bible to preach a message. The event finished at 6.45 pm. The Jesus film would have to wait.

As we ventured out to the car that evening, I noticed a boy playing a kind of hopscotch game. He was enjoying himself, content to play alone. These children were still children. I pondered the lost art of hopscotch and of many other games we played at that age. Our best friends had a farm near ours. When they had a celebration or a party, all the children and teenagers would play games outside for hours with screams and yells and exclamations of "you're out!" or "you're up!" Games like "Red Rover" or "Twos and Threes" kept us occupied and breathless until food was served. Beyond that, one could not try to resurrect these games. Everyone recognized that we had now moved on to inside games like "Snakes and Ladders" or to telling stories about funny things that happened on the farm. Sometimes, the boys got together and I was the only girl, so I joined the adults in the kitchen and enjoyed Auntie Vi's fruit cake with thick royal icing and decorative silver balls on top. This was far better. But I digress...

Returning to the hotel at 7.30 pm, Chagai, Adau and I shared chilled mango juice and Injira, while Pastor Jack went to the clinic nearby for the treatment of malaria. Although I had not eaten all day, the effects of hunger did not show themselves until late afternoon. I consumed my last protein bar knowing that I still had 10 days to go. It was impossible to know how each day would unfold. I had given up trying to have meals at the "right" time. It was normal now to eat lunch at 3.00 pm and have no dinner, just some "bisquee" (biscuits or cookies) as the Sudanese say.

I realized one day that my diet in Juba mainly consisted of egg, meat, fried potato and pasta. Interestingly, my fingernails were thriving. I looked forward to fresh fruit and vegetables in the near future, but realized that I could survive without them for now. I do recall one day though that the hotel manager had some bananas on her desk. They were from Uganda. She handed me one. I took it to the hotel room, thinking I would save it for later, but "later" turned out to be about two minutes. This would have been an organic banana and left all other bananas that I had eaten during the previous 15 years lying in the dust, so to speak. It was a true banana.

Eighteen days had passed.

13
Sunday Morning

We attended the New Site church on Sunday morning. As the service was held in the Dinka language, I had time to think, pray and observe. I looked around the room at the scarves the women wore to church and the different ways that they tied them. There were a few young women wearing wigs which gave them a Western hair style, covering their distinct Sudanese short-haired look. I did not wear a scarf. I had pondered "being all things to all people" by also wearing a head scarf, but decided to be *au naturel* unless Chagai suggested that I do otherwise. I settled for a bandana around the forehead to keep my hair in check.

Aker had said to me a few days earlier, "you look like a typical Australian". Was she referring to "Crocodile Dundee" or Olivia Newton John doing aerobics? I will never know. I thought the look might be more like "Rambo" or Bruce Springsteen, but she would not know who they were. I believe God delights in His creation and craftsmanship of hair. Whatever theology the church had about women and hair, I was careful not to give the appearance of subscribing to a "goods and chattels" mentality. Such ideologies often have one rule for the moral behaviour of men and another for the moral behaviour of women. This is an impediment to people coming to know the real God. Reverence for God was a great reason to wear a scarf... or... to not wear a scarf. It had nothing to do with the rules of man.

The microphone was suddenly handed to me without any instruction. I had no idea what they wanted me to do in the middle of the service. They probably forgot that I didn't understand Dinka. I quickly asked around "what do you

want me to do?" They said "Pray". I asked, "What about?"
but there was no clear answer. Stepping forward, I prayed
for the people, for their healing, for their ministry as a
church and for their nation.

Between the youth event on Saturday and the church
service, the youth leader gathered well over 30 names for a
youth training event on Monday. I had brought 30 note-
books and 30 custom made bags from Canada for them. The
bags were made of a distinctive fabric in brown and white.
Unfortunately, these items had been left in one of the suitcases in Melut and we could only wonder who might be using them now. Local Sudanese who were still in the Upper
Nile area said the army had been looting, when they were
meant to be clearing the area of dead bodies and making it
safe for people to return.

After the service, the people sat around outside under a
large colourful Arabian style tent. It was set up during the
morning with steel poles and sections of brightly printed
canvas, which all tied together to form one large enclosure,
open at the sides. At 2.00 pm, there would be a memorial
service here for those who died in recent fighting in the Upper Nile area. We were not required to stay for this. I sat under the tent for a while, glad of the shade while people milled
around.

Chagai brought a woman to me with two young girls.
One of the girls I recognized. She came from a village near
Malakal. When we visited the children in 2013, this little girl
was about 4 years old. She would appear by my side without
saying a word. For three consecutive days, this little girl
came to me. Each time I saw her, she stood and looked at
me with her beautiful big eyes with no expression. She
would peer into my face like she was searching for something. Perhaps a white face was the eighth wonder of the
world to her. The only time that she tried to communicate

with me was when she stood near me and pointed her finger at her feet. She was wearing black patent leather shoes. I knelt and pointed to her shoes also. Smiling at her, I told her how lovely the shoes were. Someone else might have translated, but I cannot remember. Her mother had dressed her in a very cute outfit, featuring green leggings with a matching green and white dress. If I could have taken a child home with me at that time, she would have been the one.

14
Sunday Afternoon

The taxi driver dropped me at the hotel. Mabior (not his real name), the friend and neighbour of Aker introduced himself. He said he appreciated the work we were doing in their country. He invited me to smoke something with them at the tea shop nearby. I suspect it was very similar to Cannabis. I recall Chagai saying to one of the hotel staff who were smoking the same thing, "That is very bad! Very bad!" I opted for a cup of tea instead.

He told me about the Lua tribe of central Africa and how it split into 7 groups after an incident where a necklace was stolen and the thief, a young man, was killed for his crime. The family of the young man was understandably very upset. One could see that the punishment did not fit the crime. Subsequently, the tribe split into those who sided with the family of the young man and those who sided with the people who killed him. According to Mabior, the latter group stayed in Sudan while the former was scattered to Kenya, Ethiopia, Tanzania, Eritrea, Rwanda, Burundi and probably other places. Mabior was unable to tell me about the Dinka and Nuer tribes though. Angelo, a young man smoking with Mabior, indicated that I should pay them if I want to hear the history of their people. This spoiled the whole discussion. Aker was upstairs on her balcony. While I was talking to Mabior, Aker asked if I wanted to come up and visit her. How do you talk to two people at once? I didn't know how to respond at that instant. By the time I looked up, she had disappeared.

I went over the road for "checken and cheaps" for what seemed like the tenth time (and it probably was). I secretly liked it. No surprises here except that the size of the piece of chicken varied. The chickens were definitely a smaller variety in South Sudan. Being hungry each time I ate this meal probably helped to reinforce a good eating experience like a Pavlov's dog experiment. I finished eating lunch at 2.30 pm. A partly drunk Eritrean was seated at the table next to me with Danny, one of the hotel staff. The Eritrean told me about how he worked for the United Nations for four years teaching on [land] mine awareness. His name was Keke.

Keke told me about how he had forged immigration papers for people to escape violence in Eritrea. He was arrested and imprisoned, chained by hands and feet in the dark. Later, he was released and then called up for national service and became a soldier. While out on a mission somewhere, Keke developed appendicitis, but the officer in charge did not listen to him. He began to vomit and have diarrhoea, but still they did not listen. He escaped at midnight from the army and ran away. His appendix ruptured. He prayed to God for help. The army began to look for Keke. Finally, they found him and carried him on a stretcher. Keke was sent to the nearest hospital. The doctors came to see him, one by one, shaking their heads in disbelief. They could not understand how he survived with a ruptured appendix all this time. He should have been dead. They shipped him to another location. The doctors there also came one by one to see him. They kept asking him "are you alright?" It was amazing to them how he survived his ordeal.

Keke told me he believed in Jesus Christ. Yes, he believed the story of Peter walking on the water, and then doubting. That was real, but in his opinion, some of the local pastors were not as believable as this story. His perception was that they were working for their personal gain, making the church a business. I said, "Pray and ask God to show you which church to go to, but remember that there is no perfect church."

Danny, one of the hotel staff had been sitting at the table with us. He waited for his opportunity to show me his sore eye. The left eyelid was infected. I gave him a sterile vial of eye drops to try to clear the infection or at least bring down the inflammation. I prayed for his eye for healing. I prayed also for Keke, for healing of his grief over the loss of his mother and for his spiritual growth in Christ. The bar was now a place of ministry and of fellowship around food. That's redemption.

As I was leaving the hotel, a man asked me how I had access to medicine. He saw me handing it to Danny. I explained that it is from a hospital in Canada and it was for a condition I had and that it was only a small amount for personal use. A few days later, Danny's eye had improved. The cook at the Heaven Hotel showed me a lump on her arm so I prayed for her. Adau our volunteer had headaches so I gave her headache tablets on a few occasions and also prayed for her for various ailments. The hotel courtyard was the scene of several healing prayer events. It's probably just as well that I could not understand what people were saying about me each day, good or bad. I was able to help people without the hindrance of criticism, blissfully unaware of the world like a two-year-old paddling around in a shallow pool.

Karen sent another email. She had written a "Lament to the Lord" about her journey of evacuation. I was touched that she would share it with me. It captured the sentiments of the situation very well. She hoped it would help me to "process the events and emotions" as a fellow traveller. It was true that the upheaval was difficult to reconcile in our minds, but the evacuation was so calm and quiet, there was no doubt as to who was in control. Probably what was most troubling from our perspective was the fact that so many good things were impeded or disrupted. The tension of these thoughts was resolved in Karen's last comment "Grateful that He walks with us on the Journey...wherever it may lead".

15
Exuberant Youth

The next morning, I purchased a few supplies from nearby stores and returned to the hotel looking forward to getting on with the work I had planned to do. But once more, the schedule was different than I anticipated. Chagai called to say that he and Adau were having tea around the corner at a nearby shop. We met and after reorganizing the day's schedule, we went our separate ways for the morning.

At 1.00 pm, I called a taxi and collected Chagai on the way to New Site church. The youth training session finally started with a whole slew of other people at the back of the church. Someone had opened the back door and allowed people to enter and disrupt proceedings.

I asked 3 times for them to be removed, not to be unkind, but to make sure that our work proceeded unhindered. Things were distinctly difficult today. There was a change in the atmosphere.

The connection between the projector and the generator was a very tenuous arrangement. I was nervous at the sight of bare wires being plugged into a power bar. The church was generous in allowing us to use their generator each day, but of course we provided the fuel. We purchased benzene on the side of the road sometimes. One day with no benzene in sight, Chagai paid someone to empty the tank of their motor bike so that we would have fuel. We must have paid handsomely for this for someone to be so eager to inconvenience themselves in this way, but then the Lord was providing what we needed when we needed it, so perhaps not. I was grateful that we could have electricity at all in a mud and grass church with a tin roof and a dirt floor.

I loved the exuberance of these youth. They sang songs in their own language with gusto and moved together as one when they danced. After much drumming and singing, we reviewed a typical day of the children's program. This included a DVD of North American children singing a worship song with actions. This would be their theme song for the week. How would this fly? I had asked Chagai about this in Canada and offered to show him the material, but he was not concerned. Would this translate okay into their context? Was this the worst thing that someone from the West could do? No, not at all. The youth seemed to like it. They wanted to diligently write down the words and learn the songs. We played the DVD over and over which stirred the local children to come and investigate. It was difficult to separate out one group of youth for the day. Everyone wanted to participate. The lesson was to go with it, not against it.

I talked to the youth about registering the children and taking a small group each for the week. The idea was for them to know each child by name and for the children to know they have a leader taking care of them each day. Many of the children didn't go to school so it was an ambitious undertaking to have them experience this structure. However, it was worth a try.

A card had been meticulously prepared for each child, where their name and age would be recorded. Every day, they would receive a sticker for attendance. Each day's memory verse was recorded on the card, along with the main point of the Bible message. At the end of the week, each child would take home a completed summary with all 5 stickers on a bright yellow card that they could show their family. It was meant to be a keepsake and a reminder of what they had learned. Alas, all 300 cards were left in Melut, along with the stickers. I regretted leaving that suitcase behind, but there were two reasons for doing so. First, we honestly believed that we would return in a matter of days. Second, I was concerned that if we took too much luggage when evacuating, we might be denied boarding, or may have to leave bags at the airport, unsupervised. But that was my mistake. I did not trust God to help us at the airport. He usually takes care of these details.

I asked the youth to try out the games planned for each day, so that they knew what to expect. They were reluctant to volunteer at first, but once a few brave souls had tried the first game, there were smiles and the ice began to break. Some instructions were lost in translation and the games did not turn out quite as expected, but they still had fun. The youth were patient and were accustomed to showing respect for their elders which was very pleasant and oiled the wheels of working together. We had promised the participants that a meal would be provided. It took a while to be cooked, but was finally ready by the end of the day. We finished an hour later than we estimated, but the taxi driver waited for us. I had to remind myself that some of the youth came quite a distance to attend.

16
Day to Day Challenges

On June 2nd, the first day of the children's program, we were meant to start at 2.00 pm (as if everyone wore watches!). There were no children in sight. We waited and sure enough, children began to arrive. We attempted to register each child's name and age. Instead of expensive name tags, we wrote names on squares of fabric and attempted to staple them to each child's clothing but the stapler would not work properly. Children were coming to me with sad faces because their name tags had fallen off. By the second day, we disposed of the name tags. The small groups worked for the first day, but after that the attendance of children was unpredictable. We never knew when they might turn up. I was impressed with a few of the youth leaders for their diligence with their groups. One led his group in prayer, while another invented a game with pieces of paper. There were more than 120 children present at any one time.

The next morning, I set out to buy stationery at 10.00 am, but Chagai had arrived downstairs, even though we had planned to meet at 12 noon. Pastor Jack was currently drinking tea nearby and would drive us today, which was also not what we had arranged. On the one hand, I needed to go with the flow of what was happening and who was available. Yet, on the other hand, all agreed plans had suddenly changed again without any discussion or forewarning. I had to manage the irritation of not being able to do the work that I planned to do. I needed a few minutes for the changes to percolate through my Holy Spirit filter to screen out impatience and to see through God's eyes what was happening. The Lord had decided who was driving today and when we would go and where. In a way, it protected us. No-one could predict what we were doing because we didn't seem to know either. The only sure thing was going to the church each day. Once I had processed this, I could relax and fully relinquish control.

It was a challenging day. Pastor Jack told me what he believed he was asked to do i.e. he was simply dropping me off on his way to see the displaced people. But, I needed to go to the market for supplies. I had to buy 12 large plastic balls for activities. Pastor Jack was not keen about this added task, but he accepted that it was necessary. We went to the market and found the little store that sold sporting goods, the same place where we purchased a volleyball and a football. The storekeeper was delighted that we came back, so Pastor Jack and I were each given the VIP treatment of a chair and a small can of soda while we waited for the balls to be pumped up.

On the way to the church, we stopped to buy water. The store that seemed to have everything had no water. I walked down a little side street and found a hotel that looked like an oasis, hidden away from view. There were tables, chairs and umbrellas in the courtyard outside of a pleasant dining room. The young gentleman at the bar supplied me with four well-chilled bottles of water and we were on our way.

When we arrived at the church, there was only one of the youth leaders present. I tried to set up, but there were constant interruptions by random people. I felt challenged by a lack of privacy, a lack of quiet to think and to complete tasks. The children were not accustomed to the discipline of waiting outside as requested. The youth began to trickle in. By Western standards, they were "late", and understandably so, given their transportation options and their cultural approach to time. We finally started the afternoon program about 2.45 pm.

After a while, I realized that the children's milk was nowhere to be seen and there was no sign of food cooking. People were sitting around drinking tea and having conversations. I was pushing to keep things moving through the planned activities. The woman who was arranged to present the Bible story did not show, but a pastor said he would take care of it. However, he disappeared also. It was one of those days where there seemed to be a spanner in the works. I felt abandoned.

Tea seemed to be offered to everyone else during the day, but none came my way. Each time I found a tea thermos, it was empty. I began to feel alone and discouragement was hovering. I decided to go straight to the ladies at the "kitchen" (the charcoal pit outside) and on the way, one of the women smiled and asked if I would like some tea. God is so good. He caught me up in his safety net once more. The kindly Sudanese woman delivered a tray with thermos, cup, sugar, powdered milk and spoon. What more could a girl want? What problem could not be solved by having a cup of tea?

We moved on to the theme song as everyone was restless. This always captured the children's attention. The music excited them. Young girls pressed forward doing the actions and singing. We sang the theme song every day, usually late in the day. I did not attempt to show the children the video clip that went with the music. It was too much of a distraction from the song itself. Technology should not be leaderless. It needs to be managed and used to best effect. I also wondered about the tight clothes that some of the girls were wearing in the clip. It was quite a contrast to the modest and elegant style of the Sudanese women. There was definitely a change emerging in the next generation's clothing style amongst the youth, but I did not want to interfere with their culturally modest standards as a community. Worship was the point, not fashion.

When the food was ready, the youth leaders went out with the children and helped with feeding each group. I asked the young leaders if they had eaten. They said, "Not yet. We are waiting for the children to eat first." Music to my ears. I like this next generation. I like being around them. Our transport arrived and we left the area by 6.20 pm. During the day, it seemed like nothing was working, but on reflection, there were many good things happening.

I called out to God that evening. It seemed like the men were not providing help when I needed it that day. Was it their tribal tradition that the male sits and drinks tea while the woman does the work? I thought of the book of Genesis. I don't recall only women tending the Garden of Eden. Both male and female are called to be stewards of everything, tending the garden together. I later discovered that the Dinka women do the work of agriculture, planting and tending crops, while the Dinka men traditionally herd cattle. One has to understand these things!

We were planning to give Bibles to the youth for helping us during the week. The list of names had grown from thirty as we originally requested to about forty-five. We also wanted to give the volunteer cooks a Bible each, so the next morning, we bought 100 Dinka Bibles and 50 English Bibles from the local Bible Society. We unloaded the boxes of Bibles at the hotel and stacked them in my room. The staff at the bar were asking "what do you have in those boxes?"

I said, "Bibles in Dinka and English." A hotel guest who was present asked for a Dinka Bible so it was a simple thing to give it to her. Two of the staff requested English Bibles.

We loaded the van and headed to the church at 12.15 pm. After following up yet again on benzene for the generator, I understood that we would be ready to go at 2.00 pm or thereabouts. However, when the generator was still not operating, I dared to make another enquiry. Now it was engine oil that we needed. When I think of missionaries, I think of people with great patience and the ability to work harmoniously in foreign and unexpected situations. I was unprepared for the need to follow up on logistics so frequently. There was a tendency for the volunteers to simply say "yes" when I asked a question. The word "yes" made people happy so why not use it most of the time? Instead of realizing that nothing could be achieved at this moment and letting go, I went outside and yelled (at the top of my voice) to Chagai and Deng, who were sitting in the shade chatting.

"Guys I could do with some help! We need engine oil. I will leave you to take care of it!"

If my frustration was not clear to them before, it would be now (and to everyone else in the neighbourhood.).

You have to understand that our family had a tradition of yelling when we lived on a farm many years ago. At lunchtime, my mother would stand on the front verandah and yell "Morris! Come for lunch!" Dad was in his shed working some distance away. I would estimate somewhere between 100 and 200 metres away. He would yell back "right-o!". If he delayed further, Mum would yell a second time, this time with more expression in her voice and a hint of irritation, "Morris, come on! It's on the table!" Sometimes, I was given the duty of announcing lunch.

"Dad! Come for lunch!"

"Alright, I'm coming!"

So, I had practice at this as a youngster, not realizing that it might come in handy one day.

We showed the Jesus film again as it was washed out yesterday by rain affecting the generator. The people loved to watch the miracles of Jesus and applauded each time. Some turned away when they saw the nails that were about to be hammered into His hands. Thankfully, the film did not show that detail but the people heard a loud cry of pain. Meanwhile, I took the opportunity to take a short break in the shade outside. I felt the loneliness of not understanding what everyone was saying. This was soon overshadowed by the prospect of handing out more Bibles to those eager to receive them.

I recall Chagai and I sitting in a food court in Canada in late 2014, talking about Bibles for the youth and the adults who would attend the workshop and the children's program. We estimated a figure for these and included it. Unfortunately, there were not enough funds donated for this purpose, so I had to scale the budget back at the time to only a few Bibles.

Now that the whole mission had been reconfigured, and having heard over and over how people want to do evangelism, but very few had Bibles, it was evident that this was a key to what God wanted us to do in Juba. Most of these people were displaced from Melut, Upper Nile and Baliet and probably most of those who fled left their Bibles behind, if they had them at all.

I returned to the gathering and launched into the theme song with actions. It generated such joy. It gave hope and I trust God healed the children through this. We played another song that expressed God's love for us. I wrote out the words and had them translated aloud in Dinka. This song told the gospel story. Statistics say there are many Christians in South Sudan, but I wondered how many people had been "Christianized" by a religious upbringing that did not lead to salvation.[10]

[10.] This of course is a question for every nation.

The food was now ready so we moved the younger children outside for beans and rice. A disabled girl was sitting alone in the church so we ushered her out to join the others. She was probably about 10 years old. Saliva dribbled down her chin. Her hands and legs were crooked and her movements were restricted. When the children were seated in a circle on the ground to eat, we encouraged this girl to sit down too. Once seated, she fell backwards so her legs now pointed stiffly into the air. She could not move herself back to the seated position, so another child and I rocked her back. When we did this, I noticed how her shorts were split. Her clothes were literally falling apart. After the meal, the children were as ready as ever, so we sang songs and played outside. They could not get enough of this!

At some point during the week, a thought entered my mind about running. It was about track and field. I thought about the agility of the children playing ballgames and their ability to be nimble and move quickly. Their long legs and slim, elongated build predisposed them to various sports. I asked if South Sudan had an Olympic team and wondered how they could afford to participate. I was told that South Sudan does not compete at the Olympics. The thought of the opening ceremony came to mind, when the athletes march around the stadium and carry the flags of their nations. Some countries only have one or two athletes representing them. Surely South Sudan could do that too.[11]

A national focus on sports competition could conceivably be part of the reconciliation and healing process. It would begin to draw the next generation out of the cycle of war as, together, they face their opponents on the world stage of sport.

[11.] After writing this, I saw an article posted July 15, 2015 about South Sudan's bid for membership of the Olympic Games.

I decided it was time to wind down the activities for my part, so I started laying hands on the heads of children, saying "God bless you." Before long, the children were pressing in, grabbing my hands and placing them on their heads to bless them again and again. Some came back at least 4 times. They would bring other children and position their heads so that they would be next to be blessed. I didn't know who was more blessed by this, them or me. It was a great afternoon.

I think it was this afternoon, when I noticed Chol as we were preparing to leave. He was dressed in a clean orange long sleeved shirt and a pair of long brown pants that were held up with a belt. Chol's scalp had a patchy looking skin disease. I only saw him once, briefly, while we were there. I felt such compassion for this boy. There was no spark in him like the other children. He may have had other illnesses. Who knows what he had been subjected to during the war? I was sorry that we did not see him again.

Back at the hotel, I gave Chagai and Adau some headache tablets and chilled mango nectar. Once they had left, I decided that it would be a "cheeken and cheaps" night as I had a mountain of macaroni and meat last night. A few small glucose biscuits...well, a small packet then, topped off the meal nicely. I began to work on a plan for the fifth and last day. I had a sense of foreboding about it. I knew that the verse for that day was about fear. "Don't be afraid. Take courage. I am here!" (Matt. 14:27, NLT). Usually there is a lesson to be learned and an experience that will drive home the reality of a verse like this while preparing to teach it to others. I wondered what would happen.

We tried to teach a Bible verse each day and have some consistency but no two days were the same. There were Sudanese volunteers arranged to tell the Bible story throughout the week, but they were not ready for the first day, so I took care of it. To illustrate the disease of leprosy for the children, I tore up pieces of paper and stuck them to my face and arms in random places with packaging tape. They smiled at how silly I looked and listened to the story. The adults in the back of the room seemed to enjoy it as much as the children. I don't know what the youth thought. They were probably wondering if all people from the West behaved like this. One of the male leaders taught the Bible story the next day in Dinka. I trust it went well. I have no idea. The other Bible verse volunteers never appeared. Sometimes we would have a downpour of rain that was so heavy on the metal roof, no-one could hear anything. We switched to something else when that happened, but it was not easy with one building and a gathering of children of all ages. The best move was to ask the youth to lead singing. Today, the youth leaders formed their Sudanese version of a conga line and led the children outside singing and moving forward rhythmically through the mud after a heavy downpour. The younger children followed the older children.

Amongst my end of day meandering thoughts were the observation that the laundry had not yet been returned. Three days had passed. I wondered what was taking so long. One of the staff said they had no laundry facilities at the hotel. The lady concerned would have taken the clothes home to wash and iron. The next morning, I asked her if it was difficult to do the laundry. She nodded. I mentioned that I only had a few days left before leaving the hotel. She said, "the wind". The wind? I pondered this. Is this deep and meaningful? A moment later I remembered seeing a heavy old cast iron version of an iron somewhere the previous week. Then I realized she was talking about a charcoal iron. Ah. Maybe the wind blows out the fire that heats the iron? Oh dear. It was so hard for her. Sometimes, the clothes came back almost as wrinkled as when they left. I camouflaged the wrinkles by tying a scarf around the shirt to gather it in. I may have looked like a gypsy, but a clean one at least.

17
Do Not Be Afraid. I Am Here.

We had hoped that the final day would be a grand occasion, a big finale to the week, but that soon changed. It was overcast and the clouds were very pregnant with rain. It was dark inside of the church. A young boy faithfully swept the dirt floor with a grass broom and organized chairs even though there was barely anyone around. He was an aspiring assistant. Silently, he stood by my side, holding his finger on a piece of fabric as I cut strips to make blindfolds for a game. I enjoyed these few moments together. He was fully present, eager for the next task.

Children trickled in but numbers were down. However, that did not change the level of decibels battering my ears. A few budding drummers were pounding away on drums with all their might. The youth led some worship songs and then we tackled the Bible verse and Bible story for the day. We talked about fear and trusting God. So far so good. The heavens decided to open at some point and the rain was so loud that we finally had to stop. What now?

I cleared the back half of the church and called on the youth leaders to form two teams of 5 each. I taught them a floor hockey game from Canada. We made two hockey sticks out of grass brooms. The puck was a ball of crumpled newspaper wrapped up with packaging tape. They embraced the game with gusto and competed fiercely. I had to run to shield onlookers from potential injury as the players ran after the puck in all directions, completely ignoring the boundary lines that were drawn in the dirt. Oh well, it was a new version of floor hockey. We could fine tune it later. It was meant to be a trial game for the youth leaders to teach the children, but the youth wanted to continue playing. In fact, they were lining up to take their turn. Sport was a winner.

There were one or two occasions when the youth disappeared from the building altogether. I remember being inside the church with a large contingent of children wondering where the leaders were. They were to be found outside playing volleyball. They decided to take a break. Probably a smart thing to do.

It was approaching mid-afternoon, when a volunteer came to me and said, "Sit." This was their way of saying "please take a seat." I sat in a plastic chair at the front of the church facing toward the back. There was a wooden table in front of me, with a large blackboard leaning against the front of it. A kind of low level commotion seemed to be taking place outside. I managed a few glimpses of youth wandering around. People were looking a little agitated, but it was hard to tell what was going on. I asked someone to explain what was happening. Apparently, there was a man who had fired shots in the neighbourhood. He was "upset". Someone said he was probably mad, which I guess meant mentally unstable. A few local people were running away. No-one knew exactly where the man was. I thought I saw some people laughing as if it was not a serious matter.

I was standing up when I noticed out of the corner of my eye the butt of a rifle. It was held against someone's left side at the door. The blackboard blocked out part of him. I thought this must be the deranged man who fired the shots. I sank down on one knee on the opposite side of the church behind the blackboard. I looked up and noticed a young woman sitting on a chair near the wall of the church. She was smiling, but then she looked very uncomfortable and very afraid at the same time. There were people talking but I did not know what they were saying. A little boy appeared on my left side. He was probably 2.5 to 3 years old. I placed my left arm around him and stayed there quietly not knowing what else to do. The child was completely still and did not make a sound. He could not have known what was going on, yet he did not squirm nor try to speak. Where did this boy come from and why was he suddenly beside me?

The man disappeared. Someone came in laughing and said that it was okay. I did not feel like laughing and I could not see the humor of this. People laughed at me for going down on one knee. They probably thought I was praying. I experienced the shock that they have all experienced during the past 18 months of fighting, when someone who is agitated has a gun and you don't know what may happen. I walked outside, a short distance away into the local neighbourhood.

To my left, I noticed four or five Sudanese men in police and army uniforms standing in a group, talking. I stopped when I saw them. They stopped talking when they saw me. We looked at each other. I am sure they were very surprised, almost shocked to see a white woman in the middle of this neighbourhood. I had not seen another white woman on the streets of Juba so far. There were only a couple at the airport (NGO workers) when I arrived. They stood in the same long line that I did while waiting for our passports to be stamped. I saw one white woman at Paloich airport before evacuating. It felt surreal standing out there being watched by these men. It was like walking onto the set of a movie with the story unfolding around me. Nothing I could say or do would influence the story.

The uniformed men continued to stare at me. I wasn't sure of the protocol here. I decided to walk away as I had nothing to say to them and apparently, they had nothing to say to me. They were probably discussing their response to the aggrieved man with the gun. I guess this was a sample of the "violent crime" that appeared in the travel advisory about Juba. If the Sudanese people watched the 6 o'clock news in North America, I wonder what travel advisory they might write for some of the major cities there.

Later, one of the volunteers who happened to work for national security took me by the hand and said "Helen, everything will be okay. We have this under control. The police and the army are dealing with this. It is okay." Those words sounded like reassurance from a father. The real story was that a man's cattle had been stolen and he was hopping mad. Who wouldn't be? The problem was that everyone reached for guns. Instead of seeking justice, people sought revenge. Why is that? Is it because the way of justice had failed or was too slow in the past, perhaps? This pattern of revenge that we saw with the Lua tribe and the stolen necklace keeps repeating itself. Someone steals a cow. The owner wants to kill the thief. It is part of their culture. It is tribal tradition.

I thought about what had happened and began to ask myself questions: "What brave, heroic thing should I have done in that situation? Where did that toddler come from? Should I have walked toward the man and talked to him? What would an angry Sudanese man with a shotgun do if he knew there was a white woman present? I dismissed this last thought because God had called me here and He was with me. I knew that. However, I could not escape the feeling of shock and numbness nor the feeling of guilt that I did not leap over 3 rows of chairs and stand in front of the teenage girl to protect her life. I made a mental note that next time, I can trust God even if the gunman can see me. Next time, I can even speak to the gunman. However, the truth is, if there were to be a next time, I would be just as unprepared as I was this time.

I recall one other time in my life when I was sitting opposite a man who held a rifle in his hands. It was in Australia. He was threatening to kill himself, not me. However, you can never tell what might happen. He said, "If you try to leave, I will kill myself." I don't recall exactly what happened that day, but I think we talked and he finally put the gun aside. I do recall figuring out how I would pack my belongings and make my escape within the next few days. And I did.

The latest development at the church was that the police and the army had now turned their attention to chasing cows throughout the neighbourhood. With this piece of news, we decided to resume our activities. The Jesus film in Dinka seemed to be a good choice. That would bring everyone under one roof again, but even this was doomed to failure. The projector was sending a false signal, saying the lamp was too hot even though the machine had been turned off all day. We resorted to playing our theme song, followed by another song that reached out to everyone with God's love. It seemed like this was a moment to be seized. I danced in front of a wide-eyed audience to give a very personal expression of how much God loved each one of them. I knew that many things can be lost in translation through words, so I had nothing to lose by trying to communicate through dance. It was not the kind of dance that they were used to, but I trusted that the Holy Spirit could interpret for them.

This did not feel like the last day of the program. There was no special ending. What we had done felt like a drop in the ocean. The children asked, "will you be here tomorrow?" but it was time to move on. It seemed like this was not the last chapter. The story was left open-ended. The children did not complain. Then again, maybe they were relieved that this strange person who had been invading their playground was finally leaving. They could handle it until she danced.

That was over the top, or was it the game using the blind-folds crossing the imaginary crocodile-infested river that pushed them over the edge? Is this how they live in the West? Perhaps now they could get back to their familiar game of hopscotch, something that makes sense.

18
Changing Gears

On Sunday morning, we made our way to a different part of town. It had rained heavily the night before and there were large pools of water in the streets, some quite deep. The driver detoured several times to find streets that were passable. Chagai knew roughly where we were going, but we didn't have an exact address for the church. Thankfully someone was watching out for us and noticed us one intersection away. The roadway looked too challenging, so we took yet another detour and finally disembarked from the taxi.

The yard of the church was mostly under water. The church building, (more accurately termed a shed with a dirt floor by a farmer's estimation) was full of people. My father as an ex-farmer was a great builder of sheds. He built sheds that would withstand almost anything. It was a family saying that the only things that would be left standing if we were hit by a nuclear bomb would be cockroaches and Dad's sheds. Everything was built to last. So, the sight of the timber framing and the galvanized iron of the Sudanese church was familiar to me. The only thing missing was the concrete base that usually held the posts in place.

I announced the workshop and prayed for the church. There was an eclectic mix of pastors here, all of whom had been displaced. Their own churches had become diaspora, so now they gathered together in Juba for worship. The Presbyterian way of conducting the service was very orderly. The lead pastor had a great presence about him.

Afterwards, we returned to the New Site Church for unfinished business. We gave gifts to the women who had faithfully cooked all week. They were delighted to receive Bibles and a small amount of cash to purchase some tea and sugar at the market. We did not have time to buy these, apportion them and then bag as gifts. Some youth arrived also wanting to have their Bibles immediately rather than waiting for them to be distributed by their church leaders. We asked them to wait and promised that they would not miss out. They looked quite dejected but we did not want to lose track of what was handed to whom. It did not occur to me at that time that the youth may have travelled a long distance on foot to be there in the hope of collecting a Bible. Perhaps we could have acceded to their requests but I could see a pattern developing here. Requests were beginning to sound like demands. Discernment was always needed. Was the request needing immediate attention, or, was it something to be noted for now and reviewed later? The youth did not seem to believe that we would honour our promise.

Some children had gathered outside in the meantime. I noticed a group of boys who were wheeling some toys they had made. Each toy consisted of a long stick with a wire axle attached at the end, with a wire wheel on each end of the axle. They pushed these rolling toys along the ground. They also seemed to push them and let go, maybe as a competition to see whose toy (or perhaps it is more aptly called a piece of sporting equipment) would go the longest distance? Is this a new sister sport to Canadian curling or lawn bowls? It is certainly cheaper and has zero environmental footprint. The children also played a form of hopscotch. They drew 4 large squares like a big window on the ground, and then threw a stone and hopped after it. One boy brought along a truck made of mud which was like clay. He showed it to me but only when I asked.

We returned to the hotel and walked down Tombura Road to a place to eat. We tried fish this time. In the afternoon, Bona called from his balcony "come over and hear about the Dinka/Nuer tribes". I went across and was introduced to Aker's brother, Mabior. He was visiting from overseas. Mabior was a polite young man, educated and enjoying the benefits of having his own business. He and Aker were planning to return to their family's village for a few days to stay in touch with their roots. While we were talking, a tray of drinks including half a bottle of scotch whiskey or similar arrived from the hotel bar next door. I settled for a glass of Juba Cola which I mistook for Coca Cola. The bottle was very similar to the classic coke design.

Aker reminded me of myself at her age. Hanging out with people and having a few drinks was standard practice, but on reflection, in economic terms, there was an opportunity cost. One could have been out discovering whatever it was that one was created to do and truly wanted to do in life. I didn't know at that time, that we are allowed and even called to pursue the faith-filled ideas that reside in our hearts and minds, but which alas are often buried. It takes faith, courage and patient endurance though to take that path.

Chagai advised sometime that afternoon, that a family desperately wanted to go to the Ugandan refugee camp south of Juba. They were displaced from the north to Juba and were out of food. One of the children was disabled, being unable to speak, nor walk. She had to be fed and carried. The father had been wounded somewhere between Malakal and Akoka. His leg was shattered by a bullet (or bullets) in the thigh area. He was still in Paloich but would try to travel to Juba soon. We prayed for a way for the mother and six children to go the next day. A few drivers had been contacted but no-one had responded. We both felt that it was important for them to depart as soon as possible, but there was nothing we could do for now.

The next morning at 6.00 am, Adau received a phone call from a Christian driver. He was willing to pick up the family of seven plus three others for the journey to Uganda. Around 7.00 am, I received a phone call from Chagai. "We have a driver. He is waiting at the front of the hotel." I quickly gathered the two envelopes of money that I had set aside the night before. One contained funds to pay the ten fares and the other, an amount for each person to buy something to eat and drink on the way.

There were already two passengers with the driver. They were smaller in stature than some of the Sudanese men I had met. Their clothes seemed a little too big for them, no longer a good fit. How long had they been existing on a miniscule diet? I counted the money in front of the driver and handed it to him and thanked him. Chagai asked me to pray for the two people for their journey, so I handed them the second envelope to be the caretaker of it and then prayed for their journey and their successful crossing over to Uganda.

It was an emotional time for them. They had suffered and were feeling completely helpless and powerless about their situation, but now, God had answered their prayers. They did not know what lay before them, except the fragile hope of survival for a few months in a more secure environment. They had now become like little children, totally dependent upon their father to look after them. Their vulnerability was almost palpable.

I felt the deepest compassion inside that I had ever felt in my life. One might feel pain emotionally upon seeing animals mistreated or hurt, but this was like a connection to the heart of God and what He was feeling. This farewell was profoundly moving, similar perhaps to how Jesus felt at the tomb of Lazarus. It was possibly the desperate prayers of these two South Sudanese men that had stirred the waters of the deep in another realm.

19
Another Workshop

The day was moving on. We headed to a church across town to commence our second Evangelism Workshop. The streets were gravel with large holes and gullies where the water would flow when it rained. It was a slow drive. When we were close to our destination, a sandy brown dog ran across the road with the words "THE ROCK" painted in black paint on one side of the animal. The only explanation I have for this strange sight was that the Holy Spirit was instant messaging us in a new way. He was letting us know that Jesus, the Rock, was with us. He was our foundation. He was unshakeable. The dog was both a sign and a wonder. It certainly caused me to wonder. Who in their right mind paints words on stray dogs? I don't think this was a local art project. I was too slow to capture this in a photo, but it happened.

We were the first ones to arrive at the church. It was not until 9:15 am that people began to trickle in. It was probably another hour before we could start the workshop. I had tried to explain to my church the month before how we needed to pay for transportation so that people could come to the workshops by public transport. Otherwise, they had to walk everywhere and it could take hours. Even the buses took a long time. It is difficult for Westerners to appreciate how much it meant to the Sudanese people when we provided money for some of them to take busses home. Even our taxi became a bus at day end. Several people would cram into the back seat to hitch a ride with us. Finally, we would be the last to disembark. I was very grateful when they insisted that

I sit with the driver in the front of the vehicle. I always carried a backpack full of computer gear so I needed some room. It did not always work out that way, but it was much more bearable than riding public transport with tiny windows. I looked at those small busses going by and felt suffocated just watching them.

I felt the potential for dysentery working inside once again and reached for a "Cipro" capsule. There were only two left but I trusted that I could make it through to Wednesday without any further ado. We started the workshop. Thankfully they had a large blackboard and I had brought a box of chalk with me so we were all set. My young translator seemed to grasp most of what I was saying but I will never know how accurate it was. I could only rely on others present who also spoke English and could correct his translations occasionally or assist him to find the right nuance in Dinka.

I had been advised that there would be people here making tea at 9.00 am but it did not happen until 11.45 am. Forget lunch. There was no schedule here. Food was ready when it was ready. During a break, I noticed that the cooks were preparing a quite liquid stew but no rice and the people did not use cutlery. How on earth would they eat this with their hands? Thankfully, someone had gone to the market for bread rolls.

Lunch, or whatever you call it when lunchtime has passed (post-lunch?), finally came sometime after 3.00 pm. The cooks were struggling with inadequate resources, so we took the leader of the women to the market with us on the way home that day. I walked into the store as they were discussing prices. They were telling me the cost of two large cooking pots and wanted me to pay for the goods. I was not willing to pay full price. After some discussion, the merchant agreed to give a ten percent discount. We added a tea pot and urn. As I was paying the man, the woman with us asked for additional items but we declined. It was time to go.

At some point during the day, we prayed. While praying, the issue of the water truck that had failed to deliver on time to the IDP camp at New Site came to mind, so I began to pray like this. "Lord, put a fire under these people who were supposed to deliver the water to the displaced people who had no water. That's wrong. The government is paying the drivers to deliver the water. Please send them!" One of the young women laughed when she heard this. I trust they were delighted by the picture.

We were informed that day that there was still unrest in the New Site area over cattle theft. People were fleeing. God had graciously moved us across town to another district for the second workshop. We were far away from the madding crowd, so to speak, but there were no guarantees in any part of Juba.

A volunteer with the relief society came to the hotel at day end. He had been with us in Malakal in 2013 and had defended me when a police officer tried to confiscate my camera. We were standing looking at the Nile River on the afternoon before I was due to leave the country. It was the only opportunity we had to look around so I chose the Nile River which flowed by the town. As we walked along, William (not his real name) saw a boat moving along the river and suggested that I take a photo. I held up the camera and moved it in the direction of the fast-moving boat before I snapped the shot. Unfortunately, the boat was close to where the men were bathing at that moment. Honestly, I did not see what was below the frame at the time. The policeman claimed that I had deliberately taken a picture of naked men bathing in the river below us. I was supposed to know that this is the time that they bathed each day. We were a distance away and a photo would not have revealed anything improper anyway, but this was his opportunity for quick money and he wasn't letting go.

William was short in stature but very proficient at defending rights and refusing to pay a bribe. He and the police officer countered each other with rapid-fire words, probably in Arabic.

I in the meantime held onto my purse and kept walking, pretending to be oblivious to the whole situation. We were guided to the supervising police officer's desk in a hut further along the river bank. William spoke to the supervisor and shared with him about the work we had been doing, feeding the children at Hai Salaam and so forth. The officer's heart softened and he released us. We left quickly. That was almost two years ago. When William heard that we had returned to South Sudan, he came to us in the hope of receiving assistance. His wife was currently a patient in a hospital in Cairo as a diabetic. His job as a journalist ebbed and flowed with the fortunes of the Arabic newspaper that employed him. When the newspaper printed something that the government did not like, the firm was not paid and so the staff were not paid. William's job was to report on the work of the government using the information supplied to him by ministerial staff. Lately, the newspaper was not pleasing the government and so he was in dire straits. I said I would pray and we would see what we could do to help.

20
A Surprising Conclusion

The next morning, we arrived at the church for the last day of the evangelism workshop. It wasn't until 10.20 am that we had a critical mass of people to begin. We started with the final session of healing prayer to deal with the trauma of having been displaced from their homes, fleeing for their lives and seeing their loved ones and neighbours gunned down. Today, those with recurring bad dreams were invited to come forward for prayer. One woman stepped out from her seat and was soon followed by 4 or 5 others. After prayer for the healing of memories, the workshop continued.

Later, someone asked for headache tablets. Another person said they too had a headache. I gave away the last of the Ibuprofen and promised to buy some Panadol from the market later. Soon we had a list of ailments, so I invited them to come forward for prayer. We now had about twelve people at the front. There were two kidney issues, six complaining of back pain, one with a stomach/digestive disorder, one with sciatica, one with sore legs and one unknown. I felt empty as I prayed, except that I knew the One whom I was petitioning; I knew how He had healed me, more than once.

Although the food that the women were preparing looked and smelled good, it was clear to me that I could not eat it successfully. The leader of women came to me and said, "I noticed yesterday that you were not eating. Why is that?" I explained how I had dysentery whenever I ate the locally prepared meals. The hotel food seemed to work. They had a sink for washing dishes and washing hands. The woman asked if I would eat boiled eggs. I thought they might be okay. Then she asked, "what about goat?" I thought it might be okay to try, but then changed my mind. She brought the goat anyway. She had already prepared it at home apparently and wanted me to eat it. I ate the eggs with a little uncertainty, but found them to be safe. I wondered if the giving of food might have special significance, that is, an expectation of reciprocity or "strings attached".

About 3.00 pm, we finished the workshop. We had covered what the Scriptures had to say about evangelists in the New Testament, what the Apostle Paul modelled, and even a journey through the history of conversion from the early church through to the 4th century.

Our list of workshop attendees included their language preferences. One by one, we called the participants forward by name and presented them each with a Bible. About 50 Dinka Bibles and 40 English Bibles were distributed. Arabic Bibles were yet to be purchased. The people appeared to be very happy. As each person received his or her Bible, they raised it in the air and gave thanks to God. Some of the women made a customary shrieking sound which expressed their excitement, joy and praise all at once.

Around 4.00 pm, Adau said some people outside wanted Bibles so I gave her a pile of books and went outside with her. I had no idea who these people were. They appeared to be leaders. No-one stood up or said anything. I decided it was better if she handed the Bibles out. I was not happy with the way leaders seemed to arrive last minute and asked for things that we had arranged for the workshop participants. I soon discovered that they had come to honour Chagai and I for our work in Juba. A member of the Legislative Assembly was among their number. My mistake. Once again, I needed to seek to understand from a Sudanese perspective what was going on here. Leaders had a place of honour but there was also a tribal factor tied into this that I had not yet fully grasped. In retrospect, I wondered if we should have made a special presentation of Bibles to the leaders, but the Lord did not warn me of this, nor indicate that this was needed. Chagai did not say anything either.

I noted how many of the stores in Juba displayed photos of President Salva Kiir and Dr. John Garang (previous President), side by side. Dr. Garang (from the Dinka tribe of the Upper Nile) led the Sudan People's Liberation Army (SPLA) during the Second Sudanese Civil War which led eventually to the independence of what was now The Republic of South Sudan. He was well educated, gaining credentials as a developmental economist. It was tragic that he died in a helicopter accident which had also been suspected of being an assassination. His death in 2005 was a great loss to this newly independent nation. It is particularly interesting that he studied agriculture. South Sudan was a nation of would-be farmers yet they were heading for famine once again. In a workshop in Malakal in 2013, we discussed the hope that the Sudanese had for their new nation and a key response was agriculture. At the last service we attended at the church at New Site, we prayed for successful crops for South Sudan. But I digress yet again...

A few people stood up to make comments. The leader of women also spoke. She expressed appreciation for the catering equipment that we bought for them. However, she then launched into a speech about what we will now do for them, including providing sewing machines and other support from the West. This was news to me (and no doubt to Chagai). It sounded presumptuous, but the women were delighted by it, so probably I lost something in translation through her choice of words in English. This seems to be a common practice though, whereby "thank you" speeches include cornering the guest from the West into public requests for money or other resources in a manner where it could be impolite or even humiliating to refuse.

I recall a similar situation in Rwanda in 2012. In front of the workshop participants, the leader talked about their desire for a shipment of specific books and resources. He then turned to our team leader and said they believed that we would provide what they were asking for. The same thing happened in Malakal in 2013. A public request was made of me by a church pastor in front of his congregation. We had no idea what it would cost, but it sounded expensive. The same church had decided at the last minute to charge us for the rent of plastic chairs in addition to anything else we had already agreed. If there was one thing that tended to mar our working relationships, it was this. I prayed about their request, but somehow this was not for us to fulfill. As it happened, war broke out a month later and people were either killed or scattered.

Pastor Philip was not like this. At first, I thought perhaps he would have little regard for a woman coming from the West, but what he had to say that day revealed a noble spirit with a generous heart. He gave a "thank you" speech in excellent English. He said, "I am speaking in English today, not because I have pride in my ability to speak it, but because my brother here will translate for me into Dinka in a way which will express my heart far better than I ever could." He was an orator.

I was surprised by the ceremony and official thanks. Pastor Philip expressed appreciation for the workshop and made the following comments:

"Don't think you have done little. You have done much!" He repeated this later in the speech. It was as if he had read my mail. I had wondered about this whole adventure and what difference we had made, if one could measure such a thing. He talked about what it meant to them when someone should come from the West at a time when there was insecurity, to encourage and support their people. He explained it this way.

In the Dinka tradition, the woman does not choose the man, the man chooses the woman. He pays a bride price in cows. When you see a woman whom you want to be your wife and you don't have enough cows, you will never forget the one who gives you a cow to help you. You will always remember them. He said, "You never forget that person."

"You have felt the suffering of our people and it is the love of Christ that you brought to us. We do not easily forget that."

I was moved, even taken aback, by the depth of emotion and heartfelt thanks that were expressed. The pastor gave me an opportunity to respond. The words that had been coming to mind for the last two days were "a planting for the Lord." I told them how I believed God wanted to heal them and to strengthen them at this time and that this work had been "a planting for the Lord." They invited me to return and to share the Word of God with them again.

The people began to sing and the drummers took up their positions pounding rhythmically. The pastor called Chagai and I forward and placed necklaces upon us. He tried to place a second necklace over my head, but it would not fit over the bandana, so he sat it upon the top of my head with a blue and white cross dangling on my forehead. I smiled all the way through to show appreciation, but when I looked at Chagai he was not smiling. He was looking down and very serious. Oh dear. What should I do? I noticed that the man in the front row had a broad smile on his face. Did I look funny with the necklace dangling precariously on my forehead or was he glad that I had entered the spirit of the whole event. I wondered if that meant that I could smile too. Perhaps smiling during a ceremony like this meant you were

mocking or not taking it seriously, whereas I was trying to
show a gracious attitude and appreciation for what they
were doing. If I stopped smiling and looked down at my feet,
what would that convey? That I was humbly receiving a gift,
or that I was uncomfortable or unhappy?

The ceremony ended amidst raucous praise and worship. It was a good ending, although I still wondered later
what the men thought about a woman bringing the Word of
God to them. Apparently, it was okay, but then I often wondered if it had more to do with the funds that accompanied
the visitor from the West. If I were in their shoes, I too would
be wanting all that I could for my congregation to grow in
Christ and to have resources, especially Bibles. These opportunities were few and far between for the believers in Juba.

A number of youth arrived, once again looking for their
Bibles. Word must have got out when people saw us arrive
with boxes at the beginning of the day. As we had already
told them, these were meant to be distributed by their
church leaders on the weekend. However, we had one extra
box of Dinka Bibles with us. We decided to give the youth
their Bibles and take note of their names. I didn't want them
to be turned away again. Besides, it was a fitting end to the
day. When the last box was being opened, even more people
pressed forward. It was overwhelming.

We finally left the church and walked to a nearby corner
to meet the taxi who was nowhere to be found. After about
30 minutes, I called him. He was on his way. Several people
came with us hoping for a ride, so we all stood by the road
talking while we patiently waited. Three of the youth gathered around, proudly holding their new Bibles. I asked them
about school and their aspirations. Two of them wanted to
be engineers. Moses came too, an elderly man from Malakal.
He was previously an elder with the Presbyterian Church
there. I met him in 2013. Last year, he had a stroke. He also

had surgery on his throat and was hoping to have a second operation in Cairo. Moses needed to raise USD 800 for this surgery.[12]

The taxi finally came around 6.00 pm. On the way home, the driver asked if we minded if he stopped for gas before the lines became too long. We were fine with that but had to wait about thirty minutes before we could fill the tank. I didn't really mind the wait. It was an opportunity to think about the kind of day we had and all that transpired. I was looking forward to "cheeken and cheaps" and water and maybe a bottle of that bitter lemon. That would be a good ending to my fine dining experiences in Juba at the Heaven Hotel. Something to write home about for sure.

[12.] Sadly, Moses died in August 2016.

21
Departure

I began to pack my bags the next morning. It felt great to toss some things into the garbage can. No granola bars left. No almonds. They were finished long ago. In fact, they had been a mainstay of protein for the first week. I hung on to what was left of the roll of toilet paper that I brought from Canada. So, handy. When the staff cleaned the hotel room, they sometimes forgot to bring a replacement roll. These things matter.

Ali, who had faithfully brought hot water to my room in the morning on many occasions, asked for a T-shirt. He wanted "the red one". This was a red polo neck shirt that we had printed for the functional leaders to wear with the relief society logo. There were none left so I gave him mine. He seemed happy. Now he had both a Bible and a t-shirt. The taxi came and drove Chagai, a volunteer and I to the Bible Society. We organized a gift of Bibles for three churches, but we had to have separate paperwork, so it took a while.

The Bible Society front office consisted of two tables, a couple of chairs, a display cabinet of samples of their stock and boxes of books everywhere. There were boxes of Bibles in various languages, wall to wall and floor to ceiling, but only five boxes left of Dinka Bibles. Somehow, God reserved these for us. No more, no less. This was exactly the number we had planned to buy. We added 39 Arabic Bibles and a box of English Bibles for distribution to the churches. We later discovered that they had accidentally loaded an extra box of English Bibles into the van. I asked the person in charge to add the cost to our next invoice to ensure that we paid them. There is no such thing as too many Bibles!

The leaders of the youth called Chagai later that day and said they wanted to come to the hotel at 4.00 pm and collect the remainder of their Bibles. At first, this seemed unnecessary, but later Chagai explained that they were afraid the Bibles would not reach the youth and would be passed out to others (or not passed on at all). I understood their concern and supported the arrangement. By the time we returned to the hotel, I had just enough time to finish packing, get changed and head to the airport.

Several people joined us for the journey. I needed to have a meeting with Chagai, so we sat in the back seat of the van to go over the funds I had allocated for different ministries and reimbursements. We had previously discussed many of these items in principle. I had spent time thinking, praying and preparing for this. The most important issue was to ensure that the needs that God had presented and issues that God had highlighted to us were taken care of.

I could not be there this time to pay the driver for each busload of people heading to Uganda, nor could I be there to buy resources for churches and distribute them. I trusted Chagai to carry out the remaining work, purchasing Bibles, paying the bus driver for fares to Uganda, and so on. We both tacitly understood that without this trust, there could be no effective work.

It was God who originally introduced Chagai and I through a workshop on global mission partnerships. I had just returned from a mission to Rwanda in January 2012 and happened to be in the same break-out group. Chagai issued an invitation to arrange a short-term mission with them in South Sudan. We remained in touch and by early 2013, a potential mission was being prepared. As preparations progressed, I was warned about the negative travel advisories about South Sudan that friends from church had read online. However, God had the last word. I was sitting at my desk one day at the engineering office in Vancouver when my thoughts about scheduling project team meetings were interrupted by these words: "Take a chance on me!" That was the turning point.

As we entered the chaos that is known as the check-in area, I saw that a few ladies had made the trip to the airport to say goodbye. While standing in line to collect a boarding pass, one of the farewell party asked for my shoes, not the ones I was wearing, but the ones I had locked in my suitcase. I didn't know what to do at that moment. This was not great timing. I frantically located the shoes and gave them away as I was next in line for the airline counter, but it wasn't what I really wanted to do. Another person then asked if I was leaving the laptop behind also. Okay that was enough. I could see where this was going. I felt like I was being stripped of everything.

Handling and weighing my baggage was easy on the return trip. Thankfully, the suitcases that were looted in Melut were old and donated with no expectation that they would ever return from Africa. Time was moving on. Chagai beckoned me into the line-up for the departure lounge. There were still things that I needed to tell him so we hastily exchanged a few words as the passengers moved forward. The last time I had stood here was with my poor white hat in hand and a queasy stomach. This was different. I was ready for the flight home. There was no more to do.

As I watched Juba disappear beneath us from my window seat, I felt quite annoyed with myself for giving those little shoes away in haste. It had been a confusing situation at the check-out counter, being faced with marked cultural differences awash in a sea of great need. I had been concerned about how it might appear if I said "no" at that moment. My mistake. I tried to put it into perspective, but felt swindled. This was not the work of the Holy Spirit. That's what bothered me. It was driven by something else and I succumbed to it. Apart from this, I had peace. Several of the Sudanese leaders had said to me "You will go from here and you will have peace."

22
Post Juba

After returning to Canada, I followed up with Chagai via email regarding the progress of the movement of people to Uganda. After the initial 10, a further 100 people could travel during the month of June with the mission funds that were left behind. On June 28, I received a request for a further 50 people to travel. Miraculously, there were enough funds remaining in US dollars to cover this and sundry other needs until almost every dollar was used. One pocket of money had been stuck in a Kenyan bank. It appeared that the Lord had a plan for this money. So now, a total of 160 people had passage to a refugee camp in Uganda. On July 18, I received an email from Pastor Jack (an evangelist and a regional leader). Here is an extract printed as received:

> When I was in the Refugee camp in North Uganda many peoples are Greeting you and thanking God for bring you to help transport them to the camp, a lot of Greeting to you my dear sister in Christ.

It seemed that the real issue was not the ministry that we had planned, but the answering of the prayers of the people for deliverance from harsh conditions. Perhaps I was too slow to register that. Pastor Jack mentioned at the very beginning that they were hoping to send people to Uganda, but needed to hire a bus. Most likely though, we had the right timing as I first needed to get a sense of what the Holy Spirit was doing and where the priorities lay. Along with the requests for people to be transported was the desire for six boxes (120 units) of Dinka Bibles for the refugee camp. Our faithful bus driver agreed to ship these in his van at no extra charge.

Pastor Jack's email included a further request for Bibles. Many of the refugees needed them, especially church leaders. We had arranged a box of 20 Dinka Bibles as a gift for Pastor Jack's ministry in Juba, but he distributed these to pastors at the refugee camp. He was very excited to report that he had baptized 48 people at the camp during a three week visit there, after I had left South Sudan. He wrote:

> I am so exited [excited] my dear Sister for the work [of] God because God is working now to bring his peoples back to him.

This was perfect. The Sudanese were ministering to their own people across the border. Here was a local evangelist from South Sudan sent by God to support the believers and to fan into flame the fire of the Holy Spirit in that place. The church appeared to have been scattered, but in fact, it was being strengthened in a more secure environment. Pastor Jack's plan was to evangelize "door to door" or more like tent to tent. When people have been displaced and have found their way to a refugee camp after much suffering, they are wanting to clutch onto hope, something that will make life worth living. It was so satisfying to hear what had transpired.

When making the decision to send more displaced people to Uganda, I was aware of a critical voice in the back of my mind. It evoked doubt and fear. It came with a condemning flood of thoughts like these:

"How do you know you are doing the right thing here?"
"People will criticize you for being irresponsible."
"They will never trust you again."
"You will look stupid...you are stupid."
"You don't know what you're doing."

"Your MP in Canada will be disgusted with your naivety and foolish behaviour as a citizen of Canada."

"You are interfering politically."

"You could get into trouble."

"People will lose respect for you," and on it went.

I had to lean on the fact that it was the Lord who brought this ministry to our attention, and specifically, that first family of distraught people with a disabled child. This is what He wanted. A second fact relates to how this was resourced. I had put money aside until the end, so as to discern the Lord's will. These people had been praying and asking God to send them to the refugee camp. They waited and suffered until the answer came.

I recall emailing Chagai a few weeks prior to leaving Canada asking if this mission trip should be cancelled. There was unrest in our target area at that time. I sent the email at 6.28 am on April 22nd. I remember praying with a faithful group of people from my church that morning, sometime between 7.15 and 8.30 am about this. "Lord, do you want me to cancel? Lord, I can't go unless you are with me. I don't want to go without your blessing. Please forgive me for my mistakes along the way. Lord, please make it clear." When I returned home, an email had arrived from Chagai at 8.36 am.

> Dear Helen,
> Everything is okay now in Melut but there was a fighting around Malakal yesterday. Please proceed with your trip and don't cancel it. Thank you for sharing your concern with me.
> Chagai.

Even with this unrest, God gave no indication of holding back. Even the funding of this trip testified to God's will for it to proceed. One woman had called me and said that some money had come into her hands. She thought she didn't need to keep it and it should go to the mission. As she spoke, I felt the power of the Holy Spirit coming through her words. This was a divine appointment. It was a significant amount (relative to the budget total) which made it clear that this was a "go". I only had a narrow window of about two Sundays to raise funds at my church. People were suddenly moved to give and soon the target was reached.

I recall when Chagai and I met at a food court in Vancouver to discuss details of what to include for this mission. I believe it was November 2014. We talked about t-shirts for youth leaders, Bibles for workshop participants, youth and households that sent children to us, transportation for villagers and so on. We learned in Malakal in 2013, that transportation should be provided for people to attend the workshops, but no-one responded to fund that or the Bibles specifically. I had to pare the numbers down several times and these two items (Bibles and transportation) were cut from the final budget. However, it appeared that God had another idea. He would have His way by disrupting the whole show and then allowing us to see where the pieces landed. It was truly a work of art.

We heard over and over how people wanted to do evangelism, but very few had Bibles. Most of these people were displaced from Melut, Upper Nile and Baliet and probably most of those who fled left their Bibles behind, if they had them at all.

After the army had cleared the Melut area, removing dead bodies, they declared it "safe" once more. People began to return to the town. At the IDP camp that we visited near Melut prior to evacuation, there were now 750 children enrolled at the community school, but only 8 of the 23 school teachers had returned so far. That equated to about one teacher per grade with each teacher having over 90 students. Chagai received a request from the schoolteachers for blackboards, chalk and exercise books. This was partly incorporated into a final budget which I was developing for requests received after leaving South Sudan. We added plastic sheets for the rainy season. The thought of so many children growing up in these camps bothered me. The camps were meant to be temporary, but they appeared to have become a township of their own. This was the new normal.

PART II

A MESSAGE FOR THE WEST

23
West Meets East

It was providential that our budget was flexible enough to cover so many unexpected needs. I recall a visit to the office of UNMISS on the outskirts of Malakal in 2013. While we were completing some paperwork there, I had to wait in an office for a while. One of the staff chatted with me while photocopying. He said, "The donors don't listen to us. They won't do things our way. Their money is wasted." It seemed to me that one needed to be on the ground with the local people to get a sense of what was needed and why.

On a micro level, I was challenged every day by the list of items that the cooks wanted to buy at the market. I had to seek to understand first, and then decide. I had to wrestle with providing the most basic food (say rice and lentils) over against the addition of potatoes, onions and some spices. The prices in the market were relatively expensive. One of the Sudanese had commented to me that the average person cannot afford to buy at the market anymore. There were times when Chagai and I would look at the shopping list and shake our heads. "No, that's too much. We don't need bread if we have rice." Most of the time however, we leaned toward what the cooks wanted. They wanted their food to taste good just as anyone else would. I had to keep reminding myself of their situation of displacement, and trauma and grief and that kindness goes a long way.

Purse Strings

In his book "Revolution in World Missions"[13], K. P. Yohannan contrasts the poverty of Asian believers with the affluence and wastefulness of the West. He argues that funds are better spent supporting national missionaries in Asia than sending Western missionaries who cannot speak the language, nor engage local culture the way their own people can. When Western believers fund the resources that are needed for ministry, the local pastors and evangelists can be very effective.

Yohannan struggles with the Western Christians and their stringent requirements regarding funding. He wants national missionaries to be trusted, but it is understandable that for a Westerner, there needs to be a means of tracking where money was spent and why. There is a need for accountability which builds trust. Yet we should also note the reference to this issue of trust in the book of 2 Kings.

King Joash ordered for repairs to the temple to proceed immediately after discovering that a substantial amount of money had been given for the repairs, but the priests had delayed for some unknown reason. The money was then handed over to the men appointed to supervise the work. They used the funds to complete the repair project, purchasing building materials and paying wages. However, they did not have to report back regarding where every cent was spent on this particular project due to the level of trust that existed. The Scriptures say, "They did not require an accounting from those to whom they gave the money to pay the workers, because they acted with complete honesty" (2 Kings 12:15).

[13] K.P. Yohannan, *Revolution in World Missions* (Stoney Creek, Ontario: gfabooks, 2013).

The priests handed over the money to those who were managing the project. There are believers we know whom we would trust with not only money, but with our very lives. But there may be some in our local church whom we don't know so well and to whom such trust might not be so easily extended except for a clear direction of the Holy Spirit to do so. It would be quite a stretch then, to place money in the hands of someone living in another country, working within strong tribal relationships within their traditions and culture, in a state of need, with no experience of a basic system of accountability. If a national missionary's basic needs are taken care of, training is provided and safeguards are established for success in their management and stewardship of money, would this be enough?

Another key issue Yohannan raises is the desire for control by the West of what is done in the East. It is the colonial "we know better" approach. He believes that may have been true at some time in the past, but things have changed. Foreign missionaries are no longer welcome in some countries and Yohannan says the results are simply not there. In addition to the desire for control is the kind of territorial expansion that might be related to appearing "successful", rather than being focussed on facilitating the equipping and support of locally run ministries.

He also points to Western missionaries who have set themselves up to live like kings with multiple servants attending them and their families. I personally do not know of any Western missionaries who live that way. The missionaries supported by churches that I have attended have usually struggled on low financial support and have lived simply alongside of the local people. One single female missionary I recall engaged with local drug addicts and prostitutes daily in Thailand. Raw sewerage floated by her home in the slums. She was there for the long haul and never complained about her environment. Maybe *you* know of some missionaries who live like kings? (My intention is not to call into question Yohannan's observation, but to bring an equally valid observation from another context to the table.)

How does this discussion about missions apply to South Sudan? As I see it, there are two issues here. There is 1) the issue of foreign missionaries on the ground, and 2) the issue of how to provide financial support.

Foreign Missionaries

As alluded to earlier, the local people in Juba questioned the disappearance of foreign missionaries. They argued that the United States brought the gospel but then left. They are asking for teaching, training, encouragement and support. They are not saying that foreign missionaries should not come. In fact, it's the opposite. The problem is that no-one wants to come. The Sudanese are accustomed to soldiers driving around with guns and the potential for unrest. Government travel advisories do not mean a lot to them, although they gladly acknowledge the fact that if someone from the West came to be with them at a time of unrest, it was significant. I would add that this is not a clear issue as the presence of a missionary represents a conduit to funding and resources related to their sending country. However, my experience for the most part has been a deep and profound appreciation expressed by the people for our services to them.

The Challenges of Financial Support

On each visit to South Sudan, I personally handled all finances and knew where money was spent on each aspect of the project, in conjunction with the relief society director. However, on a larger scale, funding larger and longer-term projects, there would have to be a greater measure of trust with someone on the ground. Understandably, there is a significant concern about the "big man" syndrome that prevails in such cultures. I am aware of churches who have experienced a deep sense of betrayal in this regard. In 2015, an East African leader appointed by a denominational body in Canada was removed from his post. It is believed that he failed to distribute the resources that were entrusted to him in the manner that had been agreed. Meanwhile, rural pastors under his regional purview were starving while trying to lead their churches under trees with no Bibles, and no resources of any kind.

At the other end of the spectrum, we have the local person who is blessed to have a job amid a community of hungry, unemployed people. This community will now depend on them alone for food. If this individual were to be entrusted with mission funds, the pressure upon them to manipulate those funds to support their relatives could be enormous.

Another related issue here is allegiance to Jesus Christ vs. allegiance to tribal traditions and practices. When allegiance to tribal ways trumps allegiance to Christ, we obviously have a fundamental problem. Through the recent killings and atrocities in South Sudan, it is clear that tribal ways have triumphed. As was mentioned earlier, the local pastors and leaders identified tribalism as a key concern. A major shift must take place within the wider Christian community – a shift that embodies forgiveness and that totally embraces the Lordship of Christ.

I would hasten to add that the church in the West has its own versions of "tribal allegiance". We may not be physically fighting and killing each other, but I suspect that the statistics on pornography, divorce, adultery, general promiscuity, and various addictions attest to a church that is similarly battling to embrace the Lordship of Jesus Christ fully. With regard to any of the issues being raised here, it is from a posture of trying to support and help the Sudanese church and not from a posture of finger-pointing. Those of us who live in the West, live in glass houses for sure.

I was recently informed of the "Cuban Jubans" who originated from South Sudan. They were young men of promise who were sent to be educated in Cuba. After completing their education, none of them desired to return to tribal ways of thinking. It was not possible for them to participate in tribal traditions such as revenge killing anymore. They belonged to a different society now.

So it is when the gospel of Jesus Christ takes a complete hold of us. We belong to the kingdom of God and the family of God where Sudanese stand next to Australians, Canadians, Americans and Chinese as the one people of God. This position takes precedence over culture or tradition. This is what needs to be inculcated. We are all dependent upon God's Word in the Judeo-Christian Bible to guide us in our responses to culture and tradition.

A Potential Strategy?

In 2013, we built up the local church post-war and began to equip them for evangelism. Certainly, when the South Sudanese shared their list of concerns in the workshops, two key concerns emerged:

1) Lack of funds for transportation to take the gospel to other villages; and,
2) Lack of Bibles.

It seems to me that an evangelism strategy for each church could be quantified for evangelists to be sent out to specific places at specific times. For example, a plan for a local evangelist (or small team) to travel to a nearby region for one or two weeks would potentially entail, transportation (bus fare), food and simple lodgings plus Bibles and resources for distribution, and cellphone costs. Tribes usually take in their own people anywhere, anytime so food and lodgings may be unnecessary. Leaders could agree what the basic budget needs to be. It would be relatively inexpensive.

For the most part, the local Sudanese know best what their ministry needs to be to their people. Some attention should also be paid to the basic needs of food and water and education for those who are being sent, but bearing in mind that we need to maintain parity with the local standard of living, not the Western standard of living. Our intrusion into their local economy can be harmful as many of us have learned.

It is challenging when the needs are so great. We also need to ask, what is it that we should be funding? Is the presentation of the gospel the only priority, or should it always be combined with humanitarian work such as clean water projects? Context will indicate what is required. Where people are hungry, they need to be fed or relieved in some way, especially if they are not yet believers. Where children are dying from water-borne diseases, clean water is urgent.

In South Sudan, tick "all of the above" for any humanitarian list.

There are local evangelists ready to spread the gospel and are in fact spreading it as best they can. They do not need Western Christians to be their evangelists (although we understand that God will call whomever He wants from around the globe for any task). They need support for their ministries and infrastructure for health, education and employment. We recognize that they need a reasonable measure of peace and security first before any structural investment can be made, but the gospel is to be preached in season and out of season. If lives can be saved now by providing basic water filters, then let's do that too. If the church needs to be kept alive, then let's obey the Lord when He tells us to go in with food and medicine.

Please allow me now to expound on the urgency and importance of South Sudan's needs.

24
Why South Sudan?

Predators and Prey

What we need to understand about a place like South Sudan is that people are watching. Nations like China and India are looking at the untapped natural resources of this country. One can guess that they are ingratiating themselves with the government. They are waiting for the war to end so that their plans can be implemented. As African theologian, Professor Jean-Marc Ela put it, the countries of Africa appear to be a sort of "fiscal paradise of multinationals that demand a climate of stability and security essential to the pillage of natural resources."[14] But it is not only resource-hungry nations that are eyeing what South Sudan has to offer.

Protection of Freedom

South Sudan is the newest nation on the planet. Many lives were lost in their fight for freedom and for South Sudan's independence from the north. It is imperative that the past victory is upheld.

I believe I heard a conference speaker say, "Freedom of religion is found at the foundation of every other principle of freedom". (Unfortunately, I cannot recall the name of the speaker.) A key reason why we need to support the church in South Sudan and support evangelism is that Islam (which denies freedom of religion in Africa) is pressing in upon a vulnerable and war-weary population at an increasing rate. Muslims are offering money to entice people, especially

---

[14.] Diane B. Stinton, PhD., *Jesus of Africa, Voices of Contemporary African Christology* (Maryknoll: Orbis, 2004), 35.

Christians to convert. Local pastors advised in 2015 that Islamic leaders were offering handouts to people who had run out of options to feed their families. So, what do you think those people would do? We know that once they had pledged allegiance to this ideology, they were locked into a fear-based mindset and would be targeted if they ever tried to revert to the Christian faith (or any other faith or belief). They would be entrapped by a political, legal, financial and social system that denied them freedom in every sense of the word.

If South Sudan can be taken (or re-taken) by Islam and bound up in Sharia law, the rest of Africa can be too. Can we afford to let this happen? If Islam expands beyond 15% in South Sudan, it will gather momentum and will endeavour to push through the remaining countries of Africa. Islam has the whole of Africa in its sights, not just South Sudan. The true followers of Jesus Christ in South Sudan are the beach head of resistance, the beach head of occupation. We need to occupy. We need to support and uphold the churches that are truly desiring to engage in evangelism.

Unfortunately, the Western church is slow to see that if we don't go in first, many opportunities will be lost to maintain freedom and justice. I would go further to say (as others have said) that if we don't fight the battle over there now, it will come (and is already coming) here, to the West.

We are often told in the West, Islam is a religion of peace.[15] Although we see and hear reports of horrific acts in the name of "Allah", we continue to be told by Muslims in television interviews that their religion is about peace. Nabeel Qureshi (a devout Muslim who now follows Jesus) points out that Muslims from the West "honestly report

---

[15] · Try searching "the religion of peace" on the internet.

what they believe: Islam is a religion of peace." However, Muslims from the East "will honestly report what they believe: Islam will dominate the world."[16] Clearly there is a disconnection here.

While searching on the topic of "freedom of religion", I decided to skip from the first page of Google's search results to the tenth page out of curiosity. I found an American website that challenges the argument that Islam is a religion of peace by presenting recordings of interviews with Muslim leaders, photographs and various other media. If you think concerns about Islam's agenda are exaggerated or even unfounded, http://www.targetofopportunity.com/islam.htm, may have a sobering impact. Remembering that "love does no harm to a neighbour" (Romans 13:10), we do not seek to harm Muslims (or anyone else). We pray for them and extend Christ's love to them. We see them as created in God's image as are all people on the earth. Jesus came not to condemn but to save (John 3:17) and so we keep that as our focus. As for atrocities committed against Christians (and others), we can call and should call for justice where appropriate. We also know that those who have been martyred cry out "How long, Sovereign Lord, holy and true, until you judge the inhabitants of the earth and avenge our blood?" (Revelation 6:10). The blood of every Christian martyr will be avenged at the end of the age. That's God's job, not ours.

Hearts can be hardened against our Muslim neighbours in the West, when we think of anonymous Jihadist murderers beheading men and raping women, but remember how Jesus impacted the lives of individuals like the woman at the

---

[16] · Nabeel Qureshi, *Seeking Allah, Finding Jesus* (Grand Rapids: Zondervan, 2014), 116.

well in daily life (John 4:1-42). He was face to face. He engaged under the leading of the Holy Spirit (and not according to his emotions or "good" ideas).

Remember why we are here and what the Great Commission is all about. It is about souls. Reinhard Bonnke has always talked about souls. Don't let the atrocities committed against Christians (and Jews, Hindus, Buddhists, and Secularists) at the hands of Muslim Jihadists distract us from the goal. Let's restate it here as a reminder:

> Then Jesus came to them and said, "All authority in heaven and on earth has been given to me. 19 Therefore go and make disciples of all nations, baptizing them in the name of the Father and of the Son and of the Holy Spirit, 20 and teaching them to obey everything I have commanded you. And surely I am with you always, to the very end of the age" (Matt. 28:18-20).

We need to make disciples, baptize and teach all nations to do everything Jesus has told us to do. We need to help the churches of South Sudan to not only survive, but to reach their nation for Christ and to carry out their mandate given by Jesus Christ the Lord Himself. If we do not do this now, it will affect the future of Africa.

Shouldn't we wait for peace and stability?

If we sit back and wait for this country to have peace in all areas, the end of the age will come and it will be too late. We are running out of time. There may never be peace. There may never be a completely "safe" time to go there. But there are struggling believers who are crying out to the Lord for help. God has kept them alive, but because it is a hard place, they are losing hope and falling away. Pastors are giving up and taking jobs with the government because they want to provide for their families. They want their children to go to school. After the first visit in 2013, I reflected upon this newly independent nation and saw it as a premature baby in an incubator[17], fighting for its life. This country is still fighting for its life several years later. Thankfully, they still have the will to fight.

It is easy for the West to criticize the African nations from lounge chairs in safe places. But as Christians we have to dig deeper into the news of the world. Ongoing fighting in parts of South Sudan is not an excuse to ignore the needs of our brothers and sisters in Christ. While it is a place of violence, there are still believers in that place. The churches have few Bibles, no songbooks, no children's ministry resources and no support for Sudanese missionary-evangelists.

How do you know when and where it will be "safe"?

We don't. God does. He creates the window. He leads us in the initial approach to the mission project. He manoeuvres us on the ground. He sets the boundaries.

The Holy Spirit's leading is the most important aspect of timing of missions, in partnership with local Sudanese contacts who know what is happening on the ground day by day. Prayer and discernment, while listening to various people in your church community is essential. If more than one person is saying "I think it's too dangerous, please don't go", that is not necessarily God's "no". We must follow the leading of the Holy Spirit while being open to what others around us may be saying. This topic is beyond the scope of this book, but I look forward to discussing it another time.

---

[17]. See also chapter one, last paragraph.

Needs of the local church

Due to the ongoing displacement of many people, it might not yet be the time to invest in infrastructure. However, we can invest in the discipleship of believers and support the ministry of evangelism by national missionaries.

Here are the concerns of the local believers about the church in South Sudan:

1. Lack of pastors;
2. Pastors leaving churches to work for the government so they can feed their children;
3. Islam is feeding children and paying leaders – growing fast all through South Sudan;
4. Need encouragement for leaders and churches;
5. Need training and Biblical teaching;
6. Need support of national evangelists to spread the gospel;
7. Need support for the peace process with Biblical teaching;
8. Asking for prayer for their war weary nation.

I would add to this list a matter that I discussed with at least one pastor with a church full of children. They need to repurpose their church for children's ministry and outreach through sport and games in local neighbourhoods. I believe they are called to disciple these hordes of children, many of whom are not attending school. A countless number are orphaned or separated indefinitely from their parents who may or may not be alive.

The churches are raising a key generation and need to disciple them in leadership. In June 2016, I taught on the life of Joseph and the strategic position to which he was called. We prayed for South Sudan and asked God to raise up the Josephs from this next generation as future leaders of the nation.

25
Re-Engineered Bucket Lists

One day in June 2015, I stood in a Safeway store in Vancouver, a short time after returning from South Sudan. I went there to buy two things. After walking around the store, I stopped. I looked around, feeling lost. Did I truly need anything? Not really. I felt like I was supposed to need something, but I simply did not. In the face of abundance, I had no appetite. What comes to mind is the verse that says, "Why spend money on what is not bread?" (Isaiah 55:2). In other words, why spend money on what does not satisfy? Consider how much we waste; how many resources we consume in a day. Water. Food. Energy. Commodities. Consider the unnecessary production of things that we see on the shelves of discount stores at Christmas and the amount of disposable income that is wasted spoiling grandchildren who do not need another toy, movie, cute t-shirt, chocolate bar or exciting experience (when what they really want sometimes is simply being with you). Consider the money spent on vacations that do not satisfy and do not refresh the soul as they should.

What if you said, "This year, instead of spending say $6,000 (whatever your budget is) on our family holiday, we will pray and ask God for what we could do with, say, $4,000. Let's use the remaining funds to supply Bibles to people who need them."? Picture a Sudanese evangelist distributing 300 Bibles in a refugee camp, where he has recently baptized 48 new believers. Where revival fire is burning, we need to provide more fuel for the fire and encourage it to spread. Do you believe that God can take your $4,000 and give your family a vacation to remember? When we seek God in a situation like this, I believe we can anticipate that He will open doors and pour out a blessing, not necessarily a financial blessing, but a spiritual blessing that touches our inner being and infuses us with wellbeing. That is after all what we need from a vacation, isn't it? If we listen to Him and obey, anything is possible and usually He does exceedingly, abundantly more than we could ever ask, hope for, or imagine.

As the Apostle Paul said, it is not about putting you into a situation of lack or not having what you need (2 Corinthians 8:13), especially when you need a vacation in the midst of a stress-filled life. It is about helping brothers and sisters who are in need of the fundamentals of existence, including the word of God. Then they are in a position to function in their own environment and move forward on their own. By meeting their basic needs, the church of Jesus Christ is encouraged and strengthened to shine her light in a dark place.

When believers have unmarked, disposable income, they can get ready for an adventure with the Lord, or, simply spend the money. Let's compare these two courses of action. The first option will give an opportunity for obedience, and therefore blessing. It can also be counted as a kingdom choice that may also be rewarded in heaven. Remember that the things that we do that are not for kingdom purposes and not God's desire for us are burned in the fire like chaff. However, those things that are in His service and according to His will remain like precious stones (1 Corinthians 3:13). The second option, choosing to simply spend the money with no kingdom purpose is an empty choice. (Remember also whose money we are stewarding.)

Don't leave it to Hollywood to define what is important in life. Developing a bucket list of feel-good experiences is not mandatory when you turn fifty. However, a bucket list of noble endeavours is worth considering. In 2015, I heard a conference speaker in the U.S.A. say, tongue in cheek, "if you are in a position where no-one can fire you, run your mouth for Jesus". He was speaking more to those who are at a later stage of life and can afford to spend all their kingdom currency at an opportune moment before they die. (By "currency", I am referring to the opportunities that are available to you through the network or position that you have accumulated or reached over time.) His point was that believers have something to say and need to be willing to take risks at times. Maybe there is something here for your bucket list?

As a sidebar, has God been nudging you about an issue, a letter to write to the Prime Minister, or, a public meeting you need to attend and make a short but effective presentation? I recently heard a woman from an organization named "Half the Sky Movement" make a presentation about the prevention of human trafficking to West Vancouver City Council. It was the best presentation I have heard of this nature by anyone, hands down. She had limited time, and no visual aids, just a well projected and persuasive voice and a short speech loaded with facts and evidence about the urgency and importance of the issue. It was powerful. I loved it. I wanted to hear it again. It was like a song in her that had to be sung. If she died tomorrow, she will have sung her song and left the world a richer place. I pray that God continues to use her voice in a mighty way.

Why not consider a bucket list for Jesus? If you think it's too late to make your mark for Jesus, you are wrong. Are there say 5 things you would like to do for Him? Or maybe there is one specific thing that you have pondered for a while now? Did you always want to distribute Bibles to people who needed them the most?" We hear stories or maybe read articles about believers in places like Russia or China who are desperate for even one page of the Bible. Do you want to send say, 100 Bibles to a far-away place where the people would be ecstatic about such a gift? Remember that you will meet these people in heaven and they will know what you did for them, or at least Jesus will! Do you want to send exercise books and pens to 750 children who long for education in a remote area? These things can be done quietly and efficiently and cost-effectively through trusted people. No fanfare required. No publicity. Give to those who are already doing the "heavy lifting" for you. If someone is distributing Bibles, you can support them.

There are needs all around us, but when God shows us a need, it is important to pay attention. I almost didn't go to South Sudan in 2013. It isn't that I didn't want to go, but I needed to know that it was God calling. When He shows us something with a call to action, it is an opportunity for obedience. At the end of the age, how much of what we are doing now will be burned up like chaff? Which gems will be left in the fire after everything else has been consumed? What will have eternal substance to it?

Would it not be a great thing to say, "I supported a Sudanese evangelist who spread the gospel to unsaved people in dangerous places?" Bravo! Add that one to your bucket list. If you are wondering how you can truly make a difference, if you are wanting the latter half of your life to have even greater impact than the former, then South Sudan is a potential place to invest for eternity. When children lack clean water, sufficient food, medicine, and education and live in unsafe, unsanitary conditions every day, help is needed. More importantly, these children need the gospel. In 2013, I believe the Holy Spirit gave me a picture of the faces of many little Sudanese children, captured with a lasso. God wants them in His kingdom. They are His kids. Jesus already purchased them for the Father (Revelation 5:9) and we need to tell them.

While the door is still open, it is critical to press in and press on. If Islam gains a foothold in this vulnerable nation, the doors of freedom will begin to close. One evening in June 2016, the Holy Spirit drew my attention to the public practice of prayer by about twenty Muslim men in a roadside restaurant. It was the season of Ramadan. They ate their evening meal and then prayed on their prayer rugs, taking up a significant space in that public place. We sat down at the next table, very aware of this open display of ritualistic prayer. It was almost like marking territory.

Many NGO's have retained only skeleton staff pending political stability. Yes, it is a challenging environment. However, we cannot abandon our brothers and sisters there. For want of a few resources, the gospel can be spread and believers can be baptized and discipled. There are also many people in South Sudan who have knowledge of Jesus Christ (and identify as Christian), but are not yet born again, according to a local pastor.

Someone might say "God does not send his people to dangerous places." What constitutes a "dangerous" place? Is it a place where bullets are flying? Are there no Christian war correspondents? What would Dr. David Livingstone say about this? The London Mission Society accepted Livingstone as a missionary and finally sent him to the south of Africa in December 1840. In 1841, the directors discussed a move north for Livingstone into an unoccupied district. One field representative disagreed and highlighted the dangers. Livingstone said, "If we wait till there is no danger, we shall never go at all."[18]

God began to bring David Livingstone to my attention in 2015. I had it in mind to read a book about him. Shortly after

---

[18.] C. Silvester Horne, M.P., *David Livingstone* (New York: MacMillan and Co. Limited, 1913), 25.

this, I attended a Christ for All Nations breakfast in Vancouver, where Reinhard Bonnke also began to talk about David Livingstone. Even in South Sudan, God was directing attention to the life of that missionary. Allow me to share that story.

In Juba, on June 7, 2016, I asked our driver to take me to a hotel where I hoped to connect to Wi-Fi. When we arrived, a group of women crowded around me asking for water. At first, I began to walk away. I wanted to ponder this for a few seconds. I had to consider my location and situation. A small shop was only a few metres away, so I said, "You asked for water? I shall bring water." I gave them each a bottle of water and then entered the hotel. It was best to go inside at that point and not attract any further attention.

I ordered a meal as that was usually the key to accessing Wi-Fi. Unfortunately, Wi-Fi was no longer available. Everyone had tightened up in Juba. A man came over to me in the meantime. He was a United Methodist minister wearing a large cross around his neck. He said, "I saw the kindness that you gave to those women." He began to talk about David Livingstone and his work with tribes. He said something about "when Western missionaries forget about themselves". I can't recall all that he said. Having pondered his words, he possibly meant that I could respond to the needs of the women and not be excessively concerned about safety, the money, and so on. I could be spontaneous and generous and not be bound up with what I "should" do. That would mean thinking more about the other person's need. God had my back, literally. I was in tears after the man left. It was like Jesus Himself came to talk to me. It was a profound moment. This man had such a kind face.

Circling back to the issue of dangerous places, when we read media reports of fighting, we can never tell how extensive it is. We have to dig deeper. Juba has been branded as a place of violent crime for years, yet God called us to go there on three occasions. Each time we have worked in South Sudan, we have felt relatively safe under a covering of prayer. There is a peace that passes all understanding. It envelops us. There are many who testify to the awe-inspiring protection of God in unstable places. However, we approach these things with sober judgment.

I believe God is calling for a whole new generation of missionaries, a David Livingstone generation who will go wherever God may send them, almost like marrying someone, for better or for worse. Actually, there is no "worse". Being in the centre of God's will is the safest place and most blessed place to be.

There are many good works for Christians to support, but missions change, things change. Is it time to refresh your giving strategy? How is the Holy Spirit leading you at this time?

26
Is Peace Possible?

I began writing this book about late July 2015, a short time after this particular mission concluded. A peace and reconciliation program was implemented soon after, under the watchful eye and guidance of the African Union Commission, as well as the United States. Unfortunately, and as many people expected, such an endeavour met with many challenges, not least of all the lack of authentic buy-in by the leaders of South Sudan. How can anyone generate and sustain an interest, first in a "peace process" imposed by others, and secondly in an enterprise that runs counter-intuitive to a people who were raised with vengeance deeply rooted in their culture as part of honouring one's tribal people?

The man-made peace and reconciliation formula cannot work here. It can be helpful to some extent, but it will not change the hearts of men.

Enter, the gospel. At the heart of the gospel is forgiveness. Peace and reconciliation does not work without this. As Christians, we can take leadership here by remembering God's forgiveness of us first and our vertical reconciliation with Him. This is the foundation upon which we may build a peace and reconciliation platform within a nation. The second thing to remember is that forgiveness is not optional for us. We must forgive. The power of forgiveness by Christians in dark places shines brightly.

In September 2015, I received a call to prepare a workshop on Peace and Reconciliation for South Sudan. I said, "Yes, I will go." I believed this was God's call and that He would fund it. Some continued to stand on a theology that said, "God doesn't send believers to dangerous places." Perhaps they took their cue from a few agencies who had either restricted or shut down their work in South Sudan. Other people may have been misguided in thinking that I would be trying to speak on peace and reconciliation directly to tribes who were murdering each other. "What kind of a foolish person would do such a thing? Who does she think she is?" The invitation from PLRS and the local leaders was to run a workshop within local churches. It was never about going to a battle field of bloodshed and saying "hey, stop killing each other!" No. It was always about awaiting God's gracious invitation, and carefully following His timing and procedure (Ecclesiastes 8:5).

Timing is everything. Our original departure date was April 30, 2016. However, it became clear that God was holding us back; not cancelling, but holding. Chagai's ticket was strangely cancelled by the airline due to an incorrect booking. He had to wait many days for the ticket to be re-issued and so we watched and waited, paying attention to what was unfolding. Rather than recount the whole story here, perhaps I will save that for another time, filed under the heading of "God's Timing".

The lead up to this mission was like a spy thriller story, having to outwit the enemy at each step along the way. The whole process toward the final departure was full of stress, discouragement, and rejection, but it was also full of excitement, adventure, perseverance, prayer, faith and determination to do what I believe God called me to do. And if I might add a sidebar, this is exactly what is missing in the churches of the West today. This is why young people (say under 40 years of age) are not interested in church. We have bled all adventure, faith and excitement out of serving God and reduced it to the safe and predictable. What was safe and predictable about the Apostle Paul's journeys? What was safe and predictable about Peter's mission to preach the gospel in the streets of Jerusalem? If you are not called to serve as a missionary, be careful not to stand in the way of others who are. Rather, listen to their hearts and ask God what He thinks about their audacious plans which may in fact be His plans. Both jealousy and judgment can rise up in all of us, if we allow the evil one to have his way. We must take every thought captive, examine it, and make it obedient to the Lord Jesus Christ. End of sidebar.

On this mission (2016), we managed to complete two workshops (and one overview) on peace and reconciliation, two youth training sessions and two full children's programs as well as caring for the sick and anyone else sent our way. We also handed out Bibles in two locations.

Our first workshop in Juba was attended by a Nuer pastor who lived in a Protection of Civilians Camp (POC) at the UN compound. Interestingly, this was located near a place called Mountain of the Devil or Devil's Mountain. The local people used to literally worship the devil here. This pastor was very keen to bring the message of peace and reconciliation through forgiveness to his small Nuer church at the POC. There was only one day available in our mission schedule. It was the day before I was due to depart the country. We set the date and agreed to a one-day workshop at the UN base.

I wrote earlier about the evacuation from Melut in 2015 and how James Chagai had said, "You will come again (to Melut)". Yes, we made it to Melut this time, but at first, we were turned away at the airport. In fact, we were singled out for further investigation and then told that we did not have the proper clearance. One cannot assume anything about the rules here. Things change.

We spent a full day, literally 9.00 am to 5.00 pm (excluding an absence to eat lunch), trying to obtain a security clearance through three different departments on three levels of an office building. Finally, at 5.00 pm, the very employee who had turned us away at the airport, handed us our security passes for the Upper Nile region with an imminent expiry date. These were clear boundaries. This was also an example of how God interrupted the schedule and slowed us down for our own wellbeing. It also allowed time to regroup and to think and prepare.

Upon our return to Juba from the Upper Nile, we prepared for the workshop booked for the next day at the Nuer church. Our driver left me at the gates of the UN base where Pastor Mark came to meet me. At first, we were denied entrance by the UN staff. The pastor had been given a verbal "okay" by the leader of the camp and assumed that his work was done. The UN required a letter, which is to be expected in this situation.

After two hours of going back and forth between the UN gates (by bus and motor bike taxis), we were finally allowed to enter. I was only able to speak for a few hours and then closed by praying for the sick. Half of the small community came forward for prayer and to receive any remaining medicine that could be offered. It felt to me like a Band-Aid, but the people were very happy with the visit and the encouragement. We later arranged for some Bibles in the Nuer language to be delivered to them.

There was a poignant moment at the workshop, and a very important one. An older gentleman was sitting toward the back of the church. He had been listening to me talk about forgiveness. He said, "When someone kills one of our people and we don't take revenge for that killing, we look weak to everyone. We are weak. What do you say about that?" They love to pitch a hard question. Everyone was silent. I made a few comments and cited a Scripture verse or two, and then I asked the burning question, "are you willing to appear weak as a follower of Jesus? "Are you willing to appear weak for the cause of Christ?"

I was looking toward the back of the church at this man and the people around him, but from the front, I heard a young man say, "I am willing" and then other young men say 'yes, we are willing.".

Those few words were so moving and were so humbly spoken. That right there was the heart of the matter. They were willing to lose face (and who knows what else) in front of their own tribes and other tribes by forgiving rather than killing. Amen. Hallelujah! Let's call that a "wrap"!

Every mission is different, but the needs are the same. When I left Juba, there were about 30 requests for immediate assistance in my bag. Beyond the needs of medicine, clean water, Bibles, food, clothes, shoes, eye glasses, and so forth is the need for education. This is the key for the young people of South Sudan and for the future of the nation.

27
Beyond Poverty and Politics – A Call to Action

The problems in South Sudan are complex and varied and go beyond poverty and politics. On July 11, 2016, four days after I returned to Canada, a rampage by drunk men in army uniforms took place where specifically foreign women, believed to be aid workers were raped. (One cannot tell if it was army personnel or people who happened to acquire army uniforms.) Apparently, Americans were singled out according to an Associated Press report.

A local reporter alleged that the UN staff witnessed this attack but did not intervene. Urgent messages asking for help were sent to the UNMISS base about 1 mile away, but no-one responded to their calls:

> For hours throughout the assault, the UN peace-keeping force stationed less than a mile away refused to respond to desperate calls for help. Neither did embassies, including the US embassy.[19]

In addition to this event, the UN documented over 100 sexual assault cases in Juba from July 12 to July 28, 2016.[20] Women who leave the UN compound in Juba in search of firewood or food are in danger of rape every day. The level of fear and insecurity I witnessed in 2015 has now escalated to a completely untenable way of life, as if the suffering was not great enough for these women, fleeing from one place to

---

[19]. Associated Press in Nairobi, *The Guardian*, August 15, 2016.

[20]. Aljazeera.com, July 28, 2016.

another with small children, being displaced and living in a temporary camp under duress.

I asked a Sudanese man a question about this: "Were the men who raped these women, Muslim?" His answer was "yes, they were Muslim."

There was a reason for asking this question. I had recently found on a website and also in Nabeel Qureshi's book, a reference to the Qur'an that sanctioned this particular form of violence. The author recounts for his readers how he was shocked when he discovered that Islam, his own faith that he thought he knew so thoroughly, condoned and even encouraged rape. Muslim men believe that the Qur'an gives them freedom to have sex with any woman captured by them, married or not.[21]

Muslim men take this seriously. They believe it is something that pleases Allah, or, at least has his blessing upon their participation in this. Not only that, we see evidence of this treatment of women being extended to girls as young as nine years of age.[22] I asked what action was taken about this

---

[21] The reference for this is believed to be from the Tafsir Ibn Kathir regarding Quran 4:24: "Also (forbidden are) women already married, except those (slaves) whom your right hands possess." They do not have permission, however, if the woman is pregnant. This topic is covered by Nabeel Qureshi in his book *Seeking Allah, Finding Jesus*, 242-245. It is also discussed on this website: www.targetofopportunity.com in detail.

[22] http://www1.cbn.com/cbnnews/world/2016 *Easy Meat* Britain's Muslim Rape Gang Cover-Up, August 29, 2016, Alan Hurd. This article is about "grooming gangs" that give gifts and drugs to girls aged about 9 to 14 years. The victims become drug addicts, prostitutes and sex slaves. There is a pattern of these gangs being of Pakistani ethnicity according to the article.

violence against women. He said that some of the men responsible were possibly being sent to prison and some may be executed, but there has been no news of this.

I believe it is reasonable to have asked the above question (about the identity of the men). A researcher asks questions and records data. Sometimes, we don't know if data is significant or not. It is only when we analyze the information that we begin to see a pattern. If little men in space ships come to earth and capture Labrador dogs, we would be remiss if we did not note the fact that it was only the little purple men in space ships who were doing this. The green, pink and blue men were not doing this. If no-one bothered to record this difference, key data would be lost. (We would also ask "why Labrador dogs in particular?"). So it is with asking if these men were Muslim. If there is a pattern forming over time, it is important for everyone to know that. The information should objectively be laid on the table for all to see. Whether the grouping is Muslim, Greenpeace, or Girl Guides, we need to know so that (a) we can try to understand the root of the problem, and b) justice can be administered.

Why did the United Nations not respond to the distress calls? We are still waiting for the answer. *Shouldn't there be outrage expressed by all free countries about this?* Ethiopian, Chinese and Nepalese peacekeepers did not respond.[23] Are they not peacekeepers? China's peacekeepers were noted for their diligent work when they first arrived. I noticed on July 5, 2016 that outside of the Protection of Civilians camp (I think it was POC #1), at the UN base in Juba, there was a sign indicating that China was funding the camp. China also has a keen interest in the oil resources in South Sudan. It is a tangled web.

[23.] Associated Press in Nairobi, *The Guardian Newspaper*, August 15, 2016.

Media reports say that the SPLA (Sudan People's Liberation Army, i.e. the government's military) were responsible for the multiple acts of rape. Perhaps it was Muslim SPLA members who believed it was their right according to the Qur'an? There may have been a range of motives. One Philippine witness, Gian Libot said, referring to one of the troops, "He definitely had pronounced hatred against America." He told the reporter that the soldier said, "You messed up this country. You're helping the rebels. The people in the UN, they're helping the rebels."[24] The Dinka people told me the same thing in 2015 after the UNMISS base had locked out the people of Melut who were coming to them for protection on May 19. As I mentioned earlier (chapter 8), the bodies of men, women and children who were shot by rebels lay outside of the gates. according to local Sudanese residents.

In September 2016, Mr. Jim Yong Kim, President of World Bank announced a task force to investigate sexual violence against women. I believe it is very likely that most of the use of rape as a weapon of war has been related to a particular ideology for over 1,400 years. Lack of outrage is telling. So we have a task force instead. One would hope that the truth can be laid on the table for the world to see. Yes, let it be exposed. But even if it is, it is not enough. William Wilberforce had to lobby the British Parliament for 18 years to stop the slave trade out of Africa. He did not write a report and stop there. Will Mr. Jim Yong Kim be willing to champion the cause of women (and children)? I have dim hope that he will prove me wrong.

[24.] Article at: http://www.breitbart.com/national-security/2016/08/15/south-sudan-troops-go-rape-murder-rampage

An ideology that condones rape is the same as an ideology that condones genocide is the same as an ideology that condones pedophilia is the same as an ideology that condones torture and utter brutality.

They are all condoning the destruction of humanity, one way or another. They are all condoning evil. Do we no longer recognize the difference between good and evil?

28
Are All Children Created Equal?

In early September 2015, a photograph was released by global media of a little 3-year-old Syrian boy lying dead on a beach in Turkey. His family were desperately trying to flee to Canada. Their boat overturned and 12 people died. Much was made of this tragic event. The world gasped at this, for a moment. In response, Germany threw her doors open to refugees, but 12 months later, journalists were commenting on the lack of response generally. They quoted the father of the dead boy, Alan Kurdi as saying "The photo of my dead son has changed nothing".[25]

Did you know that a similar picture was released on February 23, 2005 by New York Times journalist Nicholas Kristof? It was borrowed from the African Union archives. The photo was taken at Darfur (north of the border with South Sudan):

> ...In the village of Hamada on Jan. 15, right after a Sudanese government-backed militia, the Janjaweed, attacked it and killed 107 people. One of them was this little boy. I'm not showing the photo of his older brother, about 5 years old, who lay beside him because the brother had been beaten so badly that nothing was left of his face. And alongside the two boys was the corpse of their mother.[26]

---

[25]. Reported by Josie Ensor, Beirut in *The Telegraph*, 3 September 2016.

[26]. Reported by Nicholas D. Kristof in *The New York Times*, "The Secret Genocide Archive", February 23, 2005.

The United States Secretary of State finally and officially called this "genocide" in 2004.

There was a surge of interest around that time. Activists called for the US government to act. A documentary[27] was made in 2007 highlighting the fact that atrocities continued unchecked at Darfur despite UN memorandums and resolutions. The media made much of the little Syrian boy's photo in 2015. They ensured that the whole world knew. I am not sure if the same attention was paid to the photo of 2005. This was of a child with dark skin. Do we feel the same measure of outrage about children dying, no matter what the color of their skin may be? I hope so.

As for South Sudan's situation, as I understand it, the Islamic Arab government of Sudan is continuing with its divide and conquer strategy against South Sudan, causing ongoing strife and unrest if what the South Sudanese say is true. This is the same government that provides arms to the Janjaweed rebel forces mentioned by Kristof.

What complicates matters even further is the "non-aggression agreement" that was signed between Sudan and South Sudan. This was meant to ensure that neither will take military action against the other. It is reported that this "also prevents hosting, arming, training and providing any logistical supports to any hostile armed group operating with the ambition to advance their cause through violence to destabilize the security situation of the other."[28]

Biblical precedents indicate that there are usually consequences for signing treaties with the wrong people, or signing treaties without seeking God's counsel first. It also

---

[27] Documentary, *Facing Sudan*, Directed by Bruce David Janu, 2007.

[28] Reported in *Sudan Tribune*, October 24, 2016.

stands to reason that Sudan, being under Islamic law, will follow through on what they believe the Qur'an says, regardless of any agreement signed with a non-Muslim nation.

If we dig ourselves out from underneath the rubble of rhetoric, where do we start? In the midst of South Sudan's struggle, children are key. South Sudan's next generation has been traumatized over and over again by:

1. Witnessing unprecedented brutality and violence;
2. Witnessing death of their family members and possibly the rape of their own mother or sister;
3. Fleeing during an attack upon their village under gunfire;
4. Being separated from their families during their escape;
5. Going without food and water for long periods;
6. Being displaced from everything and everyone they know;
7. Castration – these young boys are no longer traumatized. They bled to death.

There is also the issue of child soldiers. While some are being brought out of the rebel activities and returned to society, many others are being freshly recruited. The men who do this are not held accountable. Rather, they are rewarded.[29]

A recent development puts a fine point on the pencil of this discussion. In July 2016, two days after I left Juba to return to Canada, fighting broke out. A pastor emailed me a few weeks later advising that some men from their local neighborhood had been killed leaving many children fatherless. He confirmed about 20 names, some of whom most

---

29. Reported by Skye Wheeler, South Sudan researcher at Human Rights Watch on Aljazeera.com, 4 June 2015.

likely attended our program one month earlier. There is now a weekly gathering at this pastor's church for orphans and fatherless children to play games, socialize over a hot meal and hear a Bible story. So far, it has been funded by random donors who seem to come across my path.

The children of South Sudan who lost their fathers (and others like them) need to know that they are not fatherless. They have a Father in heaven who wishes to provide for them, specifically, and give them a hope and a future. When these children pray and ask, "Father God where are you?" who are the hands and feet of Jesus to help them, if not the followers of Jesus?

Is this simply a matter of pulling on someone's heart-strings, hoping they might donate to help unfortunate children in a far-off place? I am reminded of the Apostle John's vision in Revelation 12:17 which says, "Then the dragon was enraged at the woman and went off to wage war against the rest of her offspring - those who keep God's commands and hold fast their testimony about Jesus." The enemy wants the children of Africa. He wants them either dead or deceived. This is not about heartstrings. That's too flimsy. This is war. We need to be an army of soldiers who will do what God says to do and when He says to do it. When a Christian gives a specific amount out of obedience to the Holy Spirit without delay, that act of giving is powerful in the kingdom of God. That is noted in heaven (Revelation 22:12).

South Sudan is fragile. As I mentioned earlier, it is like a child in an incubator fighting for its life. With His blood, Jesus purchased for God people from the Dinka, Nuer, Shilluk and all other tribes of South Sudan. This matters to Him.

29
Removing the Stumbling Blocks

The Missional Church

A "missional" church[30] recognizes that it is a sent church. As Darrell Guder et al. (1998) have pointed out,

> It has taken us decades to realize that mission is not just a program of the church. It defines the church as God's sent people. Either we are defined by mission, or we reduce the scope of the gospel and the mandate of the church. Thus, our challenge today is to move from church with mission to missional church.[31]

A missional church is outwardly focused. It feels like the doors and windows are open with fresh wind blowing through. The air is circulating well. When the church is open and outward, other voices are heard. Fresh vision is shared. The people are stirred within and faith rises.

Contrast this with a church that tends to be introspective and consumer-led. The by-laws might be meticulously written and adhered to, but the people are without a vision that inspires and ignites. The air is stale. Community life becomes a superficial end in itself, because the people are not galvanized toward the Great Commission. The major project that our commander-in-chief assigned to us is relegated to

---

[30.] Darrell L. Guder et al. *The Missional Church, A Vision for The Sending of The Church in North America* (Grand Rapids, Michigan: William B. Eerdmans Publishing Company, 1998).

[31.] Ibid., 6.

the status of an optional activity funded only by those "with a heart for missions".

When the church is not fulfilling her mandate, there is nothing to inspire the next generation. The baton is not passed. We become like a stagnant pool rather than a place of fresh living waters. No wonder people are leaving churches. I recall a time when a young man sold his surfboard, one of his favorite possessions, in response to a call to fund overseas missions. Another young man prayed for several years and finally was released to join the Mercy Ships ministry on the "Logos" ship. He had been inspired by guest speakers sharing vision for what God was doing in other lands. The church sent him off with joy.

The Christian Life is meant to be vibrant and deeply satisfying. We are called to be part of something far greater than ourselves. If we are maintaining the status quo and playing it safe, whom or what do we fear as God's people? Do we fear lack of finances? Do we fear offending someone because the world hates the name of Jesus? Do we fear rejection or loss of reputation? This version of Christian faith sounds more anemic than vibrant. An introspective and most likely consumer-led church that exists only to serve its members will eventually self-destruct.

An outward looking church will move from prayer to inspired vision, through discernment, to faith and into action, galvanizing and mobilizing God's people. This is where following Jesus becomes an incredible adventure fuelled by faith that all things are possible.

Unbelief

Without faith, we know quite well that it is impossible to please God.[32] I believe there are a few key stumbling blocks to becoming a missional church and at least two of these are linked to unbelief. The first is the issue of exercising faith with kingdom finances and the second is the issue of risk.

Faith and Finances

When God speaks to us about embarking on missions (local or overseas), we must not shrink back because of financial challenges. The local church will never enter her destiny if she does not move forward with what God is calling her to do. She will stagnate and possibly die.[33] Sheer demographics will win out. It is true that without vision, we perish.[34]

When God calls the church to embark on something, He will fund the vision. We only need to believe that He will provide and then do what He says. He does not ask us to do something and then withhold the resources that we need. He will give us what we need, when we need it. Has God opened doors for challenging mission opportunities for your church? Mission activity causes faith to rise. It opens the

---

32. "And without faith it is impossible to please God, because anyone who comes to him must believe that he exists and that he rewards those who earnestly seek him" (Hebrews 11:6).

33. I don't mean that the universal Christian church will die. That will never happen. I am talking about individual churches within the Body of Christ.

34. "Where there is no vision, the people perish", Proverbs 29:18, AKJV. Practically speaking, without direction, without purpose, we can be tossed by the waves like a ship at sea that finally ends up on the rocks.

windows to the rest of the world and allows the congregation to breathe fresh air. It brings the Christian journey to life.

One concern that I have heard reported for years is the issue of members of the local church channelling their giving away from their regular tithes and/or weekly offerings to fund, say, a specific mission project (or other opportunities that may catch their attention). Perhaps we could call this "distracted giving". This is symptomatic of a greater problem. Practically speaking, it is most likely an indicator of poor discipleship in the area of faith-filled and faithful stewardship.

Rather than preventing the funding of mission projects (for fear of losing weekly giving to the church), the underlying issue of what it means to trust God and to worship Him with our finances needs to be addressed. The foundation of giving as a believer needs to be established, starting with the heart. We are warned, "for a greedy person is an idolater, worshipping the things of this world" (Ephesians 5:5; Colossians 3:5). We need to remember whom we worship. We need to stay on course. I believe that God is calling "All hands on deck!" and that includes giving.

Faith and Risk

We know that church leaders today navigate a complex environment in terms of social policy, fiscal regulations, and a general proclivity to litigation in the wider community. But, do we see too much emphasis on liability concerns? Have the world's fears become our fears?[35] Are we settling for the approval of men rather than courageously going after

---

[35] "But you may suffer for doing right. Even if that happens, you are blessed. "Don't be afraid of the things they fear. Do not dread those things" (1 Peter 3:14, ICB).

God's approval? It is easy to rationalize around risk, but when God calls for action, we must hear and obey.

Are we concerned that giving financial support could mean liability in the case of injury or death, or maybe we are concerned about moral implications? That would mean that many missionaries past and present could not be supported. In what does this line of thinking have its origin? What would the Apostle Paul say about that? Did the believers who sent support to Paul think that way?

I have seen people switch from a position of faith to a position of fear through the rationalization that God will only send you when it is "safe" to go. How do we know when it is "safe" to go to a far-off country? As I mentioned earlier (chapter 24), only God knows when and where it is safe. In fact, He is the One who is able to create a safe place anywhere. God warned Joseph in a dream to take Mary and the child, Jesus and to flee immediately to Egypt. Through the spirit of prophecy, God directed Joseph to a safe place.

It was a different story for the Israelites in the book of Numbers, chapter 13. God told them to take the Promised Land even while it was full of giants. Caleb issued a faith-filled call to do it, but that generation shrank back and did not risk. John Piper writes "Caleb was unable to explode the myth of safety. The people were gripped by the beguiling enchantment of security – the notion that there is a sheltered way of life apart from the path of God-exalting obedience."[36] Both faith and obedience were necessary to take the Promised Land.

Some countries may never be "stable", but the word of God says that we are to make disciples of all nations. After

36. John Piper, *Risk is Right: Better to Lose Your Life Than to Waste* It (Wheaton, Illinois: Crossway, 2013), 35.

giving the disciples this mandate, Jesus said, "And I am with you always, even to the end of the world."[37]

When God sends a missionary, He will be with them in that place. The church is meant to pray for missionaries when they are sent. Angels are assigned. In his book "Unlocking the Miraculous through Faith & Prayer", Daniel Kolenda contrasts the fate of James and that of Peter at the hands of Herod in Acts 12. James was put to death with the sword, and now Peter was in prison, but Peter would be delivered, "as a direct result of the fervent and persistent prayers that were offered up by the believers."[38]

The Angel of the Lord was sent to rescue Peter. It was a miraculous escape. Kolenda asks "What if the church had prayed for James as they had prayed for Peter? Is it possible that the story would have ended differently?"[39] One wonders. The point is that prayer support of the church is part of the calling to the mission field. A sending church prays consistently. All things are possible when the church prays.

False Teaching, False Doctrine and the Doctrine of Demons

Another stumbling block is the proliferation of lies and deception in this age of lawlessness. We are warned that some people will fall away from true faith in Christ and follow teaching and ideas that are not of God. One version says it this way:

---

[37] Matthew 28:20.

[38] Daniel Kolenda, *Unlocking the Miraculous Through Faith & Prayer* (Orlando, Florida: Christ for All Nations, 2016), 5.

[39] Ibid., 33.

4 The Holy Spirit clearly says that in the later times some people will stop believing the true faith. They will obey spirits that lie and will follow the teachings of demons. 2 Such teachings come from hypocrites, men who cannot see what is right and what is wrong. It is as if their understanding were destroyed by a hot iron (1 Timothy 4:1-2, ICB).[40]

A lying spirit, a deceiving spirit or various other evil spirits (such as fear) can be assigned to us (or to a church) to influence our thinking. We might call them an evil spirit or we might call them a demon. They are sent by Satan (or Lucifer) to steer us away from truth and to turn us away from a direction that God wants us to take. Satan is the master deceiver and can easily blind us.

The teaching or doctrine of demons might be obviously wrong or quite subtle. An example of obvious false teaching that is active today relates to promiscuity. I have recently encountered a few professing Christians of various ages who consider that having a sexual relationship outside of marriage, i.e. that engaging in sexual immorality is acceptable to God. One brother in Christ also reported that his "Christian friends" counseled him that this was "okay". This is clearly a departure from true discipleship and what the Scriptures teach. The Apostle Paul wrote that there should not be "even a hint of sexual immorality" because this is "improper for God's holy people" (Ephesians 5:3).

A subtler false teaching would relate to what I mentioned earlier about unbelief. Sometimes, underneath a reasonable sounding argument lies a comfortable position that does not require faith, and in fact is rooted in fear. This approach allows us to sidestep the very step of faith that we

---

40· International Children's Bible.

need to take to obey God. As someone said to me recently "that's a cop-out". Discernment is needed regarding any of these potential stumbling blocks.

Mike Francen, a veteran of global outreach has written 24 books, built over 600 wells and churches in rural villages, given away 87 vehicles for ministry purposes and preached the gospel to millions. He once wrote "Any doctrine that brings about the postponement of a missionary endeavor has its origin in hell."[41]

I am not sure if I would state it exactly that way as I do not fully understand all the implications (not having the depth of experience that this man has), but I would agree that anything that tries to substitute fear for faith has to be examined and challenged. The interference of the evil one should not be underestimated when it comes to missions and outreach. Do you think our work will go unchallenged? Scripture says that our adversary knows his time is short (Revelation 12:12), so beware the tricks and subtleties that lead us away from the Great Commission.

Is Disposable Income Disposable?

The next stumbling block relates to purpose and priorities. An issue was briefly noted earlier in terms of giving to the local church. But what about our spending in general? When we study economics at high school or university, we learn that disposable personal income is a key economic indicator for an economy. It is the amount of money available to spend and save after income taxes have been deducted from household income. So, is this "disposable income" completely disposable?

---

[41] Mike Francen, *Who Will Reach Them...If Not You*? (Tulsa, Oklahoma: Francen World Outreach Publications, 1996), 33.

Why has God blessed us? According to Scripture, it is so that we overflow in good work. Some years ago, I met a couple who worked hard and ran a very successful business. They had built the house they wanted in a lovely location, enjoyed a very comfortable lifestyle and really wanted for nothing. They still had plenty of excess disposable income, but they didn't seem to have a vision or purpose except to spend it on their grandchildren. It was almost as if they were not sure what to do with this money. However, listening to one of them in the kitchen one day, I discovered that they had a heart for helping the poor and the marginalized. It seemed to me that this was God's plan and purpose for them. The excess was not meant to be spent in the world system on consumerism. It was meant to fund the redemption of all people.

The Apostle Paul wrote:

> [8] And God is able to bless you abundantly, so that in all things at all times, having all that you need, you will abound in every good work.
> [9] As it is written:
> "They have freely scattered their gifts to the poor;
> their righteousness endures forever"
> (2 Cor. 9:8-9).

The word "abound" is defined in the Oxford English Dictionar[42] as "exist in [or have in] large numbers or amounts". It was originally used in the sense of overflow or surge like a wave. The translation from Greek, *perisseuo*, includes to

---

42. https://en.oxforddictionaries.com/definition/abound

"exceed the ordinary (or the necessary)" or to be "left over".[43]

You have everything you need to do every good work; not necessarily more vacations, or more entertainment, but to abound in every good work. Vacations are good and we should be able to enjoy the fruit of our labour, but the law of diminishing returns says that the benefit derived from these things does not continue at the same rate. It will diminish. One three-week vacation per year has enormous benefit, but if there are three vacations within one year, the benefits of the second and third will be less noticeable. They may still be enjoyable, but the benefit of resting from labour will not be as marked.

Notice that it says, "in all things at all times". This is not hit and miss. This is ongoing. It is not occasional. God is saying He is able to bless you abundantly for the purpose of abounding in every good work i.e. kingdom work, lots of it.

This is the time for the church to say, "all or nothing". It's time to follow wholeheartedly, without compromise and let Jesus spend your whole life. He said to John in a vision, "To the angel of the church in Laodicea write:

> These are the words of the Amen, the faithful and true witness, the ruler of God's creation. 15 I know your deeds, that you are neither cold nor hot. I wish you were either one or the other! 16 So, because you are lukewarm—neither hot nor cold—I am about to spit you out of my mouth. 17 You say, 'I am rich; I have acquired wealth and do not need a thing.' But you do not realize that you are wretched, pitiful, poor, blind and naked. 18 I counsel you to buy from me gold refined in the fire, so you can become rich;

43. James Strong, *Strong's Exhaustive Concordance of the Bible*. (Abingdon Press, 1890).

and white clothes to wear, so you can cover your shameful nakedness; and salve to put on your eyes, so you can see (Rev. 3:14-18).

Scholars report that drinking the local lukewarm spring water could make a person sick. The lukewarmness of the Laodiceans causes Jesus to feel like vomiting. He can't stand their self-sufficiency, lack of commitment, compromise, complacency and barren busywork.

When Jesus died on the cross, it was a total sacrifice. Anyone who says they are a fully committed follower of Jesus, who has truly given their life to Him, would never be content with a nice life plus worship on Sunday. No. We are meant to overflow with good work through the employment of abundance that God has provided. Perhaps we can summarize this sub-section as simply a matter of priorities. Mike Francen speaks to this in an unapologetic manner: "Any quest worthy of your time or financial backing must weigh in eternity, and the plight of those around us. The check book of a church or individual...shows where it [she or he] is truly willing to invest, not just agree."[44]

A missional church will view missions not as a ranked activity amongst many ministries, but as their whole raison d'etre. Guder et al. (1998) note "Indeed, the main business of many mission committees is to determine how to spend the mission budget rather than view the entire congregational budget as an exercise in mission."[45]

44. Mike Francen, *Who Will Reach Them...If Not You?* 33.

45. Guder et al., *The Missional Church, A Vision for The Sending of The Church in North America*, 6.

If churches are shackled with structures that restrict the idea of missions to the work of a committee[46] hidden in a back room with an occasional report, we are doomed! As Guder et al. (1998) point out, "Neither the structures nor the theology of our established Western traditional churches is missional." If we have been stuck in our structures and theology during the last decade, we can pray today that we become unstuck, and that the Holy Spirit would blow a fresh wind upon us for change.

Blood on Our Hands?

I alluded earlier to the concern about carrying responsibility as a church for sending a missionary and a concern about unwittingly sending them to their death. The caveat mentioned earlier and throughout this book is God's call. Hearing from God and knowing personally that there is a call is paramount for any missionary. However, the church should also have clear guidance from the Holy Spirit one way or the other. Following a policy or a by-law is not in itself hearing from God. There are some who may be worried about having blood on their hands by sending a missionary, but I would like to suggest that there is another view to consider.

In 1839, the Board of Foreign Missions of the Presbyterian Church published the words of Rev. M. Macdonald who was expressing his reasons for giving up "an affectionate and prosperous pastoral charge" in London, England with

---

46. May God bless them for their faithfulness and perseverance.

the Scotch Presbyterian Church to be a missionary in the East:[47]

> I have been impressed with the consideration also, that the world is the church's trust for the express end of being evangelized...:-that for 1,800 years we have been accepting and holding this immense and awful trust at the hands of our Lord:- that at this moment there are some hundreds of millions, 'to every creature' of whom it is His clear and express command that the gospel be preached and yet to not one of them has it been conveyed by the church:-that every individual Christian, whether he own it or not, is most certainly, by his own act and deed of communion with the church, a full partaker in this tremendous trust:- that the blood of the world will be required at his hand, according to the nature of his calling, and the extent of his ability to do good:- that if there are places where this trust has been either wholly or comparatively unfulfilled, and where the Lord of all is at the same time opening a wide door for the fulfillment as in India at this time, then I am made in my own self to feel, that, of two claims or calls, I must, according to this conviction, prefer that which goes more fully to the discharge of the great and solemn trust of the whole world's evangelization.

God impressed upon Rev. Macdonald the global responsibility of the church to fulfill the Great Commission. The

---

47 · Board of Foreign Missions of the Presbyterian Church, *Foreign Missionary Chronicle*, September 1839, VII, No. 9 (New York: Robert Carter, 1839), 261; see also Baptist General Convention, *American Baptist Magazine*, May 1834, Vol. 14, No. 5 (Boston: John Putnam, 1834), 170 re the matter of blood on the hands of Christians.

minister was under conviction to answer the call. It was also made clear to him that the door was open wide to a specific nation at that time.

It behooves us to reflect upon Rev. Macdonald's letter. Does it represent missionary zeal of a bygone era or is there something of a reformation needed in the Western church today? Have we done all that we are called to do to reach our local communities with the gospel? Have we pursued opportunities while doors have been open as the letter suggests?

This is a sobering thought. On a personal level, God seems to strategically send people across my path when I least expect it. I never feel ready. When I obey such leading, there is tremendous peace and I feel emboldened for the next opportunity. About 2 years ago, I was walking a distance to where my car was parked after attending a Christian women's meeting. As I walked past one house, I noticed a man at the top of the driveway. The Holy Spirit nudged me. I kept walking asking, "Is that you Lord?" Finally, I decided to turn back and talk to the man. I walked up the driveway and said something like, "Hello, this might sound foolish to you, but I believe God has sent me here today." He had a wry smile on his face the whole time. I was still wearing my rather large name tag around my neck. He listened. I left in peace. Two things that work together here are 1) obeying the Holy Spirit (not resisting) and, 2) allowing peace to be the umpire of one's heart (Colossians 3:15).

Returning to Rev. Macdonald's letter, the world has changed since then, but the Scriptures have not. All the prophecies of the Bible continue to come true. We live in the age of lawlessness and for every day that passes, things will become more difficult. Should the church pull back in this hour, or surrender all for Jesus? What do you think?

30
Removing Lampstands

In late August 2016, I spoke to a group of people at an outreach training event. I believe God was saying at that time, "It is time to take the land." Time is running out, just as an hourglass measures the passage of time with a quantity of sand. The fields are white unto harvest, and it is important to note that the harvest will not wait forever.

I was raised on a wheat farm in Australia. Dad watched the fields closely and as they began to ripen, he checked the moisture level of the grain. As soon as a field was ready, it was harvested. We did not take our time. We did not leave things to chance such as a hail storm that could wreck the crops overnight. The machinery was ready to go. Work began early and continued through until dusk. My mother prepared food and drinks like clockwork every day. She often made deliveries to where the workers were harvesting. Everybody played their part in ensuring the crops were harvested efficiently and at the right time. We find in the teaching of Jesus on the kingdom of God, a direct reference to this idea of harvesting as soon as possible: "As soon as the grain is ripe, he puts the sickle to it, because the harvest has come" (Mark 4:29).

One day in September 2016, my thoughts were interrupted with these words, "lampstands will be removed." I pondered this and at first, I thought about the reference to lampstands in the book of Revelation. John wrote that he saw "someone like a son of man" standing amongst seven golden lampstands. Jesus revealed that "The seven stars are the angels of the seven churches, and the seven lampstands are the seven churches" (Revelation 1:20). Subsequently, in the letter to the church at Ephesus, as instructed by the Lord, John wrote,

> 4 Yet I hold this against you: You have forsaken the love you had at first. 5 Consider how far you have fallen! Repent and do the things you did at first. If you do not repent, I will come to you and remove your lampstand from its place. 6 But you have this in your favor: You hate the practices of the Nicolaitans, which I also hate (Rev. 2:4-6).

In that context, Jesus commends them for their diligent work and perseverance, but there is a serious issue He must address. He calls for repentance and action. The lampstand (or church) will be removed if there is no repentance. This may be interpreted as a church being taken out of commission altogether.

When the words "lampstands will be removed" first came to mind, it was in the context of harvest. A few weeks earlier, I had written out what I believed God was saying about the need for outreach and that the time was now. It is conceivable that if the Lord did indeed shut down a church, whatever harvest fields were under the stewardship of that church, they will now be given to another church who will take action to reap that harvest. Whichever way we may approach it, this appears to be a warning. We need to pay attention to what God is saying and I believe it is in the context of the harvest. Jesus can remove lampstands. I believe He will be doing that if we do not heed His call in the coming days.

In Closing

In the early 90's, Brenda Salter McNeil visited a church in Birmingham, England as part of a team of African American seminarians and church leaders. Their tour was in partnership with the Oxford Centre for Mission Studies. They were met by a large group of young Jamaican residents. When the meeting began, Brenda's team were immediately confronted by a young woman who loudly demanded answers to these questions:

"Why didn't you come sooner? "

"Didn't you know what we were going through?"[48]

Brenda describes her reaction to this:

"We had been absolutely clueless...we hadn't realized that there were people in other countries around the world who needed us."[49]

God sent Brenda and other leaders at that time to hear the cry of the Jamaican people in that city and location.

When God sent me to South Sudan, I could not ignore what the Christians said during the first workshop, "Nobody is helping us. You send a message to the West."

Is your church shrinking back and withering within four walls? Are the windows closed and the air stale? There are people out there who need you. Which cry is coming before you? Which cry reaches your ears?

Ask God to open the doors and windows while there is still time. Let the Holy Spirit blow a fresh wind. Repent of failure to act, delayed obedience and unbelief. Ask the Lord of the harvest to breathe new life into your church and to show you the bigger vision that He has for all of you. Which harvest field (or fields) has He parcelled out to you? What will you do about that and when?

---

48. Brenda Salter McNeil, *Roadmap to Reconciliation*, (Downers Grove, Illinois: Inter-Varsity Press, 2015), 12

49. Ibid., 13.

Finally, remember the advice of Frederick Buechner who wrote, "The place God calls you to is the place where your deep gladness and the world's deep hunger meet."[50] Find that place. When God sends you out, follow His travel advisory closely, paying attention to every detail.

Peace be with you.

---

[50] Frederick Buechner, *Wishful Thinking: A Seeker's ABC* (San Francisco, California: Harper Collins Publishers, 1993), 118-119.

Afterword

Whether travelling for business or pleasure, one must heed travel advisories. You usually need to do that anyway to meet insurance requirements. Respect the government's work of keeping the movement of people relatively safe around the world. Please do not be foolish. Please do not be presumptuous either. Remember how Satan set Jesus on the pinnacle of the temple and then tempted him to throw himself down, and how Jesus responded (Luke 4:9-12). We do not put the Lord God to the test in that way.

However, when God is calling you to travel and others are also involved in your arrangements, as I was with PLRS as my hosts, then you need to be aware of the travel advisories and factor them into your deliberations about how God is leading at the time.

Each time I have gone to South Sudan, I have had a certainty mixed with faith in my mind and heart about how God has led me and others. That strong sense of call enables me to face the challenges that inevitably arise. There are others much more experienced than I in these areas, but I hope that this may be useful advice.

Pray with others. Talk to your pastor. There is no shortage of great mission opportunities around the world, but time is moving on, so start praying!

What about You?

Death is inevitable.

When we stare death in the face, there is no time to go back and ask questions about the hereafter.

People research house insurance. They may go online to learn about the side effects of a prescription drug. They study a travel guide to figure out the best way to go in a strange country, but much less time is devoted to knowing what will happen when they die.

The Bible tells us a lot of interesting things about this, but the outcome depends on a choice that we make while still alive. So, what is the choice? It is basically a choice between life, as in eternal life, or, death. Please allow me to explain briefly. Death is not simply sleeping forever. There is no "Nirvana" or some other place where "good" or "nice" people go and "rest in peace". No. There is first a physical death, followed by judgment and then a potential "second death" in a lake of fire. To be avoided!

Eternal life means living forever in a realm of no more tears and no more pain. It is a place of joy and peace that surpasses our earthly experiences of these things. Earthly bodies subject to decay are changed into immortal bodies like those of the angels. Can you imagine? At the very end of the Bible it says, "He will wipe every tear from their eyes. There will be no more death or mourning or crying or pain, for the old order of things has passed away" (Revelation 21:4).

How do we gain access to this place? Jesus Christ is the only One who can take you there. The Bible tells us in several places that if you believe in your heart in Him as the Son of God, and say that with your mouth, you will be saved. A verse from the book of Romans says it this way: "That if you confess with your mouth Jesus is Lord, and believe in your heart that God raised Him from the dead, you will be saved" (Romans 10:9).

The question you might ask, then, is why did Jesus die? Very briefly, all of mankind has fallen short of the holiness of God. Adam and Eve (whom God formed as the first man and woman) had a choice to obey God, but Eve was deceived, sin entered the world and so we lost relationship with God the Creator. Many curses came upon us and made life difficult.

The good news is that Jesus Christ was sent to bridge the chasm between us and His Father in heaven. Jesus is the only One in the history of the world who died for all mankind, to save us from that second death. He is the only One. When you accept Jesus as Savior, you have assurance of salvation, that is, of being saved from condemnation for your sin, and being forgiven and made right with God. That's the truth right there. There is no guesswork. The body of Jesus was resurrected. He returned to heaven and one day He will return to earth.

Be assured that when you receive forgiveness from Jesus, you need never fear death. Eternal life through Jesus Christ will give you an inheritance in heaven of far more than you could ever hope for or imagine.

If you want to have peace from today on about going to heaven when you die, then pray this prayer and commit your way to Him for the rest of your life:

"Dear Lord God,

Thank you that you have provided a way for us to know you personally.

Thank you for sending Jesus, your Son, to die for my sins. I receive your forgiveness for all my wrongdoing. I receive Jesus Christ into my life as my Lord and Savior.

Thank you for the gift of eternal life.

Please heal me of things that have hurt and wounded me. Please break the chains of bondage and all curses over my life.

I ask in the name of Jesus Christ. Amen."

If you prayed that prayer, please email me and let me know. This is the beginning of knowing God. You need to connect with a pastor as soon as possible. I can make suggestions for how to go about that if you don't know where to start.

Be assured, friend, that the true God loves you so very much. That's unconditional. Does Jesus want you to enjoy heaven with Him? Absolutely!

Enquiries

Helen Miller
P.O. Box 51553 Park Royal RPO
West Vancouver BC V7T 2X9
Canada.

Please join the mailing list:
https://goo.gl/UBrnpc
(This is the best way to keep track of what we're doing.)

Email: ChildLike@missionagogo.com

Facebook Pages:
@lovesouthsudan   (mission)
@helenmillerbook   (book updates)

Blog: http://wp.me/P76hoO-1
(Note: This is currently a blog for general readership, not specifically Christian, but may change.)

Webpage for this Book: https://goo.gl/JYCLgi

One Last Thing

Thanks for reading! If you enjoyed this book or found it useful, I'd be very grateful if you'd post a short review on Amazon, https://www.amazon.com/
or, at https://www.amazon.ca/ .
Your support really does make a difference. I will read reviews personally so I can note your feedback. Thanks again for reading!

Made in the USA
Columbia, SC
28 November 2017